What
It
Takes
To Heal

PRENTIS HEMPHILL

What It Takes To Heal

How Transforming Ourselves Can Change the World

Cornerstone Press

1 3 5 7 9 10 8 6 4 2

Cornerstone Press
20 Vauxhall Bridge Road
London SW1V 2SA

Cornerstone Press is part of the Penguin Random House group of companies
whose addresses can be found at global.penguinrandomhouse.com.

This is a work of non-fiction. Some names have been changed
to protect the privacy of the individuals involved.

Grateful acknowledgment is made to Little, Brown Book Group Ltd for
permission to reprint 'Song for the Old Ones' from *Maya Angelou: The
Complete Poetry* by Maya Angelou, copyright © The Estate of Maya Angelou
2015. Reproduced with permission of the Licensor through PLSclear.

First published in the US by Random House, an imprint and division of
Penguin Random House LLC, New York, in 2024
First published in the UK by Cornerstone Press in 2024

www.penguin.co.uk

A CIP catalogue record for this book is available from the British Library.

ISBN: 9781529935639 (hardback)
ISBN: 9781529935646 (trade paperback)

Book design by Susan Turner

Printed and bound in Great Britain by Clays Ltd, Elcograf S.p.A.

The authorised representative in the EEA is Penguin Random House Ireland,
Morrison Chambers, 32 Nassau Street, Dublin D02 YH68

www.greenpenguin.co.uk

MIX
Paper | Supporting
responsible forestry
FSC
www.fsc.org   FSC® C018179

Penguin Random House is committed to a
sustainable future for our business, our readers
and our planet. This book is made from Forest
Stewardship Council® certified paper.

To my great-grandmother Odessa Manson,
for passing down the word

To Amaya, Chaston, and Miles—may you always be
free enough to say what you know

CONTENTS

A revolution involves making an evolutionary/revolutionary leap toward becoming more socially responsible and more self-critical human beings. In order to transform the world, we must transform ourselves.

—GRACE LEE BOGGS,
Revolution and Evolution in the Twentieth Century

INTRODUCTION
TO THE UK EDITION

IN MARCH 2018, WHILE ON A TRIP TO LONDON, I WAS INVITED, along with a few other US-based community organizers, to visit Grenfell Tower. This was already nine months after the devastating fire that killed seventy-two people and displaced hundreds more, many of them migrants to the UK. Still the tower haunted, an imposing emptiness, hollowed of life. I remember how eerily quiet it seemed; its windows blackened eyes looking back at me. Paper heart cutouts draped the fence and underpass across the street. A makeshift memorial collected prayers for the lost and surviving. It had been a raging, rapid fire, I was told, that caused the carnage, but it was something else, which had settled over the building long before, that set the stage for that summer night. An absence of care, a neglect, by the owners of the building and local officials who had refused to heed the safety warnings, the pleas from the tower's inhabitants.

The organizer who'd brought us there led us around the

corner from Grenfell to what was, on the outside, an un-
assuming building. Yet, inside was a space that vibrated with
life. Children ran in and out through the maze of rooms, chasing
one another and laughing. Against the walls were pallets filled
with jars and boxes of food for families in need. We were shown
rooms where survivors received free therapy sessions and we
saw fliers inviting tenants to regular meetings there, where they
could address concerns and organize. It was organic, flourishing with all that had been missing at the site of the tower. It was
clear from the space that, somehow, their community was still
there. Community, I wrote later in my journal, is made in part
by proximity, the shared experience of living in one place, but it
is also made of something much more ineffable. Community, at
its core, is who you are willing to care about and for.

Afterward, we sat down to lunch with some of the families who had survived that night yet still lived with the after-
math. They told us stories of uncertain living in hotels, the
government's continually delayed response, of feeling invisible and unheard, and the years of organizing by Grenfell residents that had predicted the eventuality of this disaster, even
if they couldn't prevent it. I was surprised. I had assumed,
naïvely, that living in a country with nationalized healthcare,
one that seemed to provide so many basic supports in contrast
to my own, meant that people there had social safety nets.
That some entity would step up on their behalf and provide
for them when tragedy set in.

With the fire, people had lost their homes, and with them
their belongings. But not only those. They had lost their short
commutes to work, their trusted schools, the heartfelt conversations with their neighbors, the grandmothers who watched
their children when they had an errand to run. And, with the

trauma of the fire ever present in their minds and their bodies, they had lost their ability to rest and recover. The community center had given them belonging, a place in the world to come together and just be. To talk and grieve, to remember, to move forward, to be heard, to demand safe housing, to say "Enough." It was a place to heal.

What I saw that day at Grenfell and in the building next door, I have seen replicated in my home country and around the world. When traumatic events or daily oppression implode lives, people ache to find a way to heal in communion with others. To heal by tending to our minds, bodies, and souls, and by transforming the systems that caused harm in the first place. When trauma impacts us—and it touches some of us with more frequency and force than others—we need to be held by these communities that nurture and sustain us.

Wherever we call home, we have a front-row seat to mounting crises around the globe, from the economic to the existential. Wherever we look, we see fracture and polarization, and we feel overwhelmed. We don't know how to respond, whether there's something we can do, or if there's any point anymore. It is in these times of discord that we must remember that, as humans, there is more that connects us than divides us. Our circumstances, our hardships, no matter where we live, bear an uncanny resemblance to one another's, and instead of allowing them to drive us further apart, we need to find a path toward connection. Now, more than ever, is the time to commit to building a world where all of us can thrive, where we strive to understand one another, where we can tend to our trauma and push for more just systems and policies. A place where we create spaces for all of us to feel and breathe and flourish. A community of care. This is what it takes to heal.

BEGINNINGS

WHEN TRAYVON MARTIN WAS KILLED, I HAD JUST STARTED WORK-ing at a community mental health clinic in Los Angeles, one of three Black therapists on a staff of nearly fifty. Most of the clients assigned to me were Black, mostly queer, mostly working-class, and mostly people who had never seen a therapist before. It was the reason I became a therapist in the first place: I hoped that people like me could sit across from someone like them and say the things they'd held on to for so long. I'd been in therapy myself for several years before I ever worked with someone who mirrored my identity in any way, and, most important, because of that mirroring, held my experiences with a certain weight and tenderness. It was a relief when it happened; I could let go of the extra effort it took to translate myself while at the same time trying to feel what was newly emerging. Suddenly, words it had never been safe enough to even form could be spoken.

There's something revolutionary about creating a space

for people to lay down what burdens them. We can carry our pain like a secret. We learn somewhere along the way that we are to blame for our own hurt, our shame, the feeling that we don't belong. We bottle these secrets up, push them down, because we don't have the time or space to look them in the eye or to fall apart. We find ways to cope, drowning our histories in substances or overwork, but we forget how, over time, the past and our efforts to stifle it erode our focus, our ability to be present, and our sense of power and agency in the world. Concealing this pain wears down our capacity for vulnerability and connection, and eventually our bodies, too. Our stories need airing out and places to land. Whenever my clients at the clinic shared something of their pain with me, I knew that it was often a rare moment of expression, that they might hide their feelings again as soon as they left my room, but they might breathe just a bit easier, too.

Trayvon's name came up with nearly every one of my clients in the time between his death and the acquittal of the man who killed him, George Zimmerman. Trayvon was innocent. A young man caught in the crossfire of something set in motion a long time before him. One client, a mother, came in that week worried for the safety of her children. Trayvon's murder had prompted *the talk,* the one given to Black kids about how to make their bodies less of a provocation for the violence some are waiting to inflict. I had received some version of it myself. Don't talk back, give them what they ask for, leave with your life. She was terrified to know the warped way the world looked at her babies, and furious, too, that they were never seen as precious outside of her arms. Another client, in her thirties, remembered her favorite cousin who was now gone, also killed as though his life were meaningless.

She told the story through her tears, wiping them with force before they could fall. He was murdered by someone who looked like him, another young Black boy, but the root, she said, the hatred of Black people, was the same. At the end of another session, a man on the edge of middle age, who had come to see me with his wife for couples therapy, put a hand on my chair and asked, not looking me in the eye, if I had heard what happened to that boy. "It's a shame how they do us," he said and shook his head.

All the stories I heard at the clinic were different but linked. Individually experienced fears and feelings of grief were interwoven and overlapping, connected by race but specifically by history. By the great lie, told first to justify colonization, theft, and kidnapping and to protect the teller from the truth of what they had allowed to happen, of what they were allowing themselves to become. The lie that claimed that Black people were subhuman, the lie that justified profiting from our bodies, that always found a way to render our early deaths acceptable, if not inevitable.

I felt that same fear and grief, too. There was something about Trayvon's face, his smile, that forced me to feel. It reminded me of boys and young men I knew and had known. Bright, mischievous, sweet. Like Oscar Grant, who worked at my local grocery store in Oakland before he was killed on the Fruitvale BART station platform, face down. And Emmett Till, in photos buttoned up and smiling before they destroyed him.

When I looked at Trayvon's photo, I saw an innocence, a budding, beautiful Black boy with Skittles and an iced tea in his hands, headed home from the convenience store, talking to a girl on the phone. I saw myself. I remembered walking down Southern streets in my own teen years. I was fifteen when we moved to a new neighborhood, into a house with two showers, green grass in the yard, and, for the first time, a room of my own. It was the first house my mother had ever bought, the one that gave us a place away from the abuse, and the nicest one I'd ever lived in. That first day, the Black family across the street came out to greet us: two parents, four boys, and a girl who seemed to be my age. While the parents spoke, we kids stared at one another, deciding. The girl broke the line first and asked if I wanted to walk with her to get ice cream. My mother nodded her approval, and I followed the girl down the street. We walked four blocks exchanging questions about our schools and our friends. It felt like the teen novels I spent every summer reading, moving into a new home, a new neighborhood, and finding an instant best friend. It really felt like a new beginning. Like freedom.

Two blocks from the ice-cream shop, a white man swung his porch door open, charging at us, red-faced, mid-scream, "You niggers need to leave this neighborhood now!" I stood there unable to move for a second before my new friend grabbed my arm. "Come on!" We ran without stopping all the way back home. To someone watching, we might have looked like we were playing, two Black kids, heads pushed high, racing down the middle of the street, but this was not that. We were running in terror, too scared to look over our shoulders in case that man with his red face was close behind. It's not that I hadn't encountered the vitriol of racism before. I had, often, at school and in town. But I had never felt that specific fear in my own neighborhood before, so close to home.

When we got back, I was shaking.

We told our parents and they scooped us up and we retreated to our homes, but my mother didn't ask many questions of me or say very much at all. I imagine she wasn't
surprised; she knew what the world could do. Having grown
up in segregated Louisiana, she may have had too many of
her own stories of running scared to think there was any use
in comforting me. I didn't know exactly because she'd never
said—perhaps she'd never been given the room to.

The girl and I never got our ice cream that day or any
other, and we hardly spoke to each other again. Somehow
what had happened seemed the fault of us coming together,
of imagining that we could just be kids who got ice cream on a
summer afternoon. I never ventured past the end of our block
after that. I was terrified of what lay beyond, of the violence
my Blackness seemed to activate in others.

THE DAY AFTER ZIMMERMAN WAS ACQUITTED, it felt like the walls
of the clinic wanted to burst. Fifty-minute sessions couldn't
contain the rage and grief. There was grief and rage in my clients, and there was grief and rage in me. It was all I could do
to maintain my composure, to act like a "therapist" and resist
pushing open every door and bringing us all together to cry it
out in the hallways. That week's meeting with our clinical supervisor was devoted to how we might support our Black clients around the verdict. It agitated me, not because it wasn't
needed, but because it was clearly not enough. I wanted healing for my clients and every Black person everywhere that day.
I knew how much we needed it. But I was starting to sense
the limit to what we could do as therapists, that as much as

each client needed room to heal and tell their stories, the people who came to see me each week needed the world to change, and not just how they felt about it.

It's hard to heal when you're still being hurt.

There was something disingenuous about trying to fit each client's emotion neatly into personal therapeutic rooms when what they were feeling was never only individual. We needed, I thought, to be willing to step outside of these rooms and into the world, in a way that involved and maybe implicated all of us.

After the verdict, Los Angeles shut down. The whole city erupted in protests, and I went straight from the clinic to the streets, anxious to be with people who were willing to call out injustice and name what needed to change. I had planned to meet up with friends who were already marching, but I was late after seeing clients, so I parked my car just off Crenshaw Boulevard and started walking between the bodies of people. It was a warm night with an edge in the air, music and sirens blending into a chaotic mix, but more than anything there was a kind of beauty in this spontaneous gathering of people who were here because a boy had been taken from us. People with signs stood on corners and shouted, "No justice, no peace," getting hoarse from the repetition. There were people clustered in parking lots, edging into the road, generations of families walking together. Occasionally, a wandering group of young people entered the intersection and stopped traffic or jumped on the hood of a cop car, and then a line of police with riot gear pushed the crowd back to its banks. But we weren't afraid. That night the streets belonged to the people. It was my first protest after moving to Los Angeles, but it's a city that reminds you that it is built on the fault lines of past eruptions. Watts, the uprisings and riots in response to the beating of Rodney King and the murder of young Latasha Harlins, all of it was there in the air that night.

It was electric. One of those rare moments in life when you can feel the raw power that exists when people come together. It felt like everything could be changed right then and there, and the presence of armored police vehicles somehow only confirmed this feeling. I walked through the streets in my work shoes and a tucked-in Oxford shirt, my therapist's uniform. I opened the top buttons to breathe a bit easier. After a day of bumping up against the limitations of therapy, I needed this, this reminder that we could and should be able to shape what happens to our lives and our communities. We were restoring a sense of our power that is lost in violation. It was its own kind of healing. I'd been drawn to organizing at the tail end of my time in undergrad, searching for belonging and meaning and a way out of the feeling of futility. It had given me that, the sense that we could do something to change things. As much as I wanted individual therapy for every one of my clients, I wanted them to have this feeling, too.

Yet, after my day of hearing and holding clients' stories I was tuned in to another current running through the air that night. I could feel, even here, woven into our chants and written on our signs, the same pain that had spilled out of my clients earlier in the day. I walked past a woman leaning against a car who was wearing a shirt with airbrushed wings and dates displaying the complete life span of someone young whom I imagine she had loved. Someone gone too soon. I saw again how connected we all were by those stories we held, by our grief for our dead. We had come to march for justice, angry at systems that had broken generations of our people, that still murdered boys like Trayvon and refused him his innocence. It was painful how many stories we all held, how everybody had a ghost. I walked among people I didn't know and yet knew deeply. As much as this was a march for justice, it was a march for people who had lost people. It was a protest against a world that made it seem as though it didn't matter. I was back at the question that brought me to therapy in the first place: What are we going to do about all this grief?

The next night a group of activists shut down the 405 freeway and brought L.A. traffic, and therefore L.A., to an utter standstill. It was everywhere on the news. Afterward, my friends, who were local community organizers, invited everyone from the streets who was interested to meet back at their spot. A couple hundred of us gathered in an art studio in St. Elmo Village, an artist community just off La Brea Avenue. It would become the first meeting of the Los Angeles chapter of Black Lives Matter. We were there because we knew something needed to be done and we were ready to do it. Finger paintings of Brown children covered the walls. We shifted boxes of art supplies and scrunched our knees under the short, circular kids' tables. The room moved and buzzed, people spilled outside onto the sidewalk, peering around the corners to listen in on what was being said. Everyone greeted each other: "What's your name? Where you from? Glad you're here."

None of us knew exactly what was happening, but we knew it had never happened before.

Patrisse Cullors, a local organizer, opened the meeting with a huge, warm smile. "Welcome, everybody. It's so beautiful to see all of your faces here. We're going to do some dreaming together tonight for what comes next. For Trayvon and all the people we've lost." People nodded and rumbled their commitment. The room was divided into smaller groups, and each group was assigned core conversations: One large group huddled to devise the next protest; another was talking about how to keep us safe in the streets. Most of the people there clamored toward the action. I was asked if I would facilitate a conversation on healing justice. I was nervous. I'd always been most comfortable behind the scenes, but this conversation in this moment was the culmination of everything that had been on my mind. Plus, there was something about being with people with shared purpose that made me more courageous that night. I stood up and wrote the words "healing" and "justice" big on a piece of paper and held it up high in the corner for people to find me. Just twenty or so people made their way to my table, moving in close to hear one another over the hum of the room. We were one of the smaller groups, and I could tell that none of us knew exactly what it was we were being tasked with.

I had only one question: "What will it take for us to heal?"

The term "healing justice" was one many of us had started to use as a way of understanding the role of healing in social movements. It came from a framework offered years earlier by Cara Page, a healer and an organizer who had worked in the South and had come to understand that our spiritual and healing practices had always been necessary to our survival, and that our care for one another had always been political. The work that Cara and the Kindred Southern Healing Justice Collective had done was an inspiration for many of us who had similarly found our way to these questions of care and healing and what they had to do with the freedom we'd been talking about for so long.

When I was asked to facilitate the conversation that night there was still so much I was trying to understand. I had pursued justice and healing work as separate solutions, but I was beginning to realize how deeply interwoven they were, how one enriched and made possible the other.

That night standing in front of the butcher paper on the wall, I asked our gathered group what healing meant for us now. What it meant against the backdrop of George Zimmerman's acquittal for the murder of Trayvon, what it meant as we entered the streets to shut down a system that refused to let the boy be innocent, that refused to acknowledge that what brought us into the streets was love, grief, a desire for things to change. The answers came back clear and cascading. A woman near me offered that we needed churches with no walls, places of Black worship outdoors that didn't turn any of us away. I remember writing "churches with no walls" and feeling floored by the beauty and clarity of the statement. Churches that weren't a place of exclusion but a place of discovery. It was overwhelming to feel the possibility. "We need therapists for everybody," another person near me shared. "Spaces to be joyful!" "We need food in our neighborhoods." Meditation centers. Living wages so people didn't die early from stress and overwork. Nature camps for our children. Access to healthcare. To be able to grieve in public. Every answer felt more like a revelation and an affirmation that social change at its best made room for well-lived lives. I was stirred in my core writing the responses on the wall. This question I'd been asking, "What will it take for us to heal?" wasn't a question that took us away from serious social change. It was a question that showed us where we were headed and how to get there, what it could feel like. What was being proposed wasn't just social change or isolated healing, but both, at the same time.

IN THE DECADE SINCE THAT first meeting, as I've worked with many organizations and many different people, I've been trying to put the answers to this question into action. I stayed involved with Black Lives Matter as it grew from a hashtag to perhaps the largest social movement ever, with a network, at its height, of forty-two chapters. I joined the staff as healing justice director in 2016 and worked there until I left in early 2018. In some ways, my job title was aspirational. We knew that healing was crucial in social movement work, but we weren't exactly sure of how best to go about it. Still, knowing the profound effects that therapy had on my clients, that sense of relief they felt when they opened up and shared, I was determined to figure out the connection. Formally, my job was to provide support for local leaders of the different chapters of BLM as they, in turn, supported people in their chapters and communities with emotional and interpersonal challenges. I provided counseling, internal conflict facilitation, and grief support. I led a working group of BLM members from across the country—Philadelphia, Long Beach, Cambridge, and Sacramento—creating tools for other chapters navigating conflict and mental health crises. These included meditation, acupuncturists, pop-up clinics, days of rest, and retreats to process the trauma so many of us experienced in our lives and that flared as we took to the streets. We had new language, but these offerings were reminiscent of interventions from earlier times, the Black Panther Party's community clinics, the social safety net of church, all the way back to the grief circles and herbalism of enslaved Black people. But as BLM continued to explode in numbers, as pressure mounted from the media, and as those who were part of the larger movement navigated threats, caring for ourselves and one another often got pushed to the side. There was so much that we wanted to do, so much that others needed us to make happen, and as the network was pulled in a million different directions, politically and structurally, sometimes it was hard to remember the shape of our visions. The story of that time is yet to be fully told, but it seemed for all of us that it was an immersive and at times overwhelming lesson in what it takes to make significant change in the world, on personal, interpersonal, and societal levels, what works and what gets in the way.

Over time, I have come to understand that social transformation (the push for more just systems and policies) and personal transformation (healing our own trauma and reshaping our relationships) have to happen together. Not one or the other, but both. We neglect ourselves or our growth in our rush to change what is external. When we do, we fracture, and succumb to what we are unwilling to face.

BY THE TIME WE GOT to the summer of 2020, we'd found out that Ahmaud Arbery had been hunted down and killed while jogging, Breonna Taylor had been woken up from sleep and shot to death in her hallway, and George Floyd had died with his head on the pavement and a man's knee in his neck. With this string of brutal killings amid a pandemic that highlighted racial injustice and healthcare inequity, people and corporations seemingly stepped up. I had never seen anything like it. They made massive pledges for racial justice, darkening social media feeds in solidarity, promising money and trainings and restructuring. Every company had a BLM banner on the front page, and every white influencer was passing the mic and their platforms to Black spokespeople. Suddenly the issue of police violence was in the forefront of everyone's mind. It seemed that the years of protest had finally cracked through a layer of collective denial and inaction, that the work of organizers on the ground was making a difference. Everywhere I looked, people seemed ready and willing to make change.

But when the seasons shifted, not much else did.

The pledges for money—in the billions, the media reported— never made it to small Black businesses, the trainings hardly happened, and the killings that had outraged people over the summer kept their pace through the fall. White support of Black Lives Matter dropped to its lowest level on record. It seemed as if everyone had come to the edge of the precipice, held hands, but failed to jump. The change that was needed required more than many were willing to give.

We are not far from that eruptive moment. It is still calling on us to change. The world as we know it is in an ever-escalating state of collapse. Much of what has seemed solid—institutions, cultural mores, global power relations, and even our weather patterns—is decaying or morphing into something unfamiliar and potentially devastating. Reactionary and oppressive movements are building. Racial justice has for a long time been at the forefront of conversations, and is requiring a new kind of action, less performative and more material. The #MeToo movement illuminated gender-based violence, revealing the extreme degree to which sexual abuse and harassment have been normalized in our society. But while high-profile celebrity cases were exposed, we still struggle to address this violence in our everyday, more intimate relationships. The Covid-19 pandemic has shown us the inadequacy of our institutions to meet our needs. Our systems are flawed and failing, and more than a million Americans died, a disproportionate number of them Black, Brown, and Indigenous. Technologies are rearranging our economic realities, distracting us and disturbing our very sense of who we are. Climate change threatens all of us on earth, not in some distant future, but now, as severe weather across the globe has shown us again and again. And yet many of us, our countries, and our leaders remain entrenched in consumerist, fossil-fuel-focused cultures. Chaos is a constant, terrifying us with its uncertainty. But the chaos offers something else, an opportunity for recalibration, realignment, and reshaping. This moment is ours for the taking. So many of us are ready to step up, but how do we move over the edge? How do we take action knowing that what we face is bigger than what any individual can handle alone?

In family systems therapy, the term "transitional character" refers to the person in a family who takes on the work of interrupting and changing generational patterns. We become who we are in part because of the family system that shaped us, but we can become even more of who we are when we resist, when we take a look at where we're from, where we want to go, and then begin to transform our future. It's a fascinating concept to me not only as a therapist but also as someone who has tried to take on this role in my own family and in community organizing. I believe we can decide to transform every system in which we are embedded—our families, our communities, our places of work, our schools, our organizations, our institutions—if we seek out and are given the support to heal and act.

This book is written for the *transitional characters* of this moment, for the changemakers. Those feeling stirred by what's going on in the world and who want to get involved but are overwhelmed by the idea or unsure. Those who are already involved in change work, brought to it by wanting to end injustices that have happened in their own lives, and exhausted by facing the trauma again. Or those who see how the culture of change work itself has replicated some of the patterns around exclusivity and shaming that they wanted to address in the first place. None of this is easy. The moment calls for more than changing a social media banner or blacking out a feed. It is calling for more than a public pledge. The kind of change we are after is cellular as well as institutional, is personal and intimate, is collective as well as cultural. My goal in writing this book is to support the people who are courageous enough to face the complex uncertainty of this time and who want to make a difference, to choose life, authenticity, connection, and joy. It is a guide to show how we can become people who can live with more feeling, more balance, and more power, to point us in the direction of solutions, and to give us what we need to show up.

I didn't know what would come of my own journey with healing and my own journey with social change. When I started both I was overwhelmed at times, frustrated, lost. But through the beauty of what I found in me and in other humans around me I learned some things that I think are critical lessons for the times we are facing, and they make up the chapters of this book:

- **Vision:** The first step in any change is imagining that something else is possible for you and for the world. Recovering our ability to imagine what doesn't yet exist and committing ourselves to what we envision are what carry us through the hardest moments.
- **Heal:** We must be engaged in healing our trauma. Our lives can then be enjoyed and lived more fully and with more feeling. Otherwise, our best efforts for change fall apart when we have not done our work.
- **Feeling and the Body:** To embody change means that our declarations are more than good ideas, and our actions become more than performative. The change we seek unsettles our patterned ways of being, and our truest values become what we practice.
- **Remapping Relationships:** Skillful relationships are the bridge between our individual transformation and systemic transformation. More than we realize, history and power script our relationships with one another and prevent the kind of reciprocity and connection we need to heal ruptures between us. If navigated well, our relationships become a powerful foundation for the liberation we seek to create.
- **Engage with the World:** We have to be engaged in the work of changing the big systems that we each operate inside of. Healing and self-care on their own are not solutions to what we face. And our coming together to change things changes us—it heals us collectively.
- **Expanding Our We:** Many of us hold narrow ideas of who *we* are. Much of what lies ahead is the work of expanding our we and learning to relate to one another, not as we've been taught, but with a new future in mind.
- **Things Fall Apart:** Our greatest challenge is to not allow our ruptures and breakdowns to become new sites of trauma

for one another. We need skills to navigate our conflicts and crises with groundedness apart from the reactivity of our times.

• **Change Is a Process:** Change doesn't often happen in one big event; it's the everyday work and risks we take to make something happen.

• **Courage:** Courage is needed in both private and public moments to take risks that change the course.

• **Love at the Center:** When we have love at the center of what we do and how we do it, it expands belonging and safety and makes change worth the effort.

I'm grateful to take what I have learned amid change and share it with you, to accompany and support *your* healing and leadership. Through my own personal experience and my work as a therapist, an embodiment teacher, and an organizer I came to see that our bodies hold our stories, and it is through the body that we have to heal. My hope is that in doing so, we move toward our best visions and dreams for healing our relationships with ourselves, with one another, and with our planet.

It sounds big, but like everything, it starts small.

What
It
Takes
To Heal

1

VISION

Without new visions we don't know what to build, only what to knock down. We not only end up confused, rudderless, and cynical, but we forget that making a revolution is not a series of clever maneuvers and tactics but a process that can and must transform us.

—ROBIN D. G. KELLEY,
Freedom Dreams: The Black Radical Imagination

IN THE FOURTH GRADE, WE WERE ASKED TO STUDY A FIGURE we admired in early American history and present a report, dressed as that person, to the class. The assignment came from my teacher, Ms. Jefferson, a tall, thin, middle-aged Black woman with a bootleg British accent who looked down on you over the rim of her glasses. I knew, though no one else in the class did, that she lived in the same hood as me, just two blocks away in a pink brick house with a manicured lawn. Over the summer, my dad had pulled some strings, made some calls, so I could be in her class. I was being sent across town to a majority white school and I wanted a Black teacher. The year before I'd had the only other Black teacher in the school, Mrs. Williams. She smiled when I spoke, hugged me tight into her neck, asked me what was wrong in private when I came to school upset. She was a home to me.

It only took a couple weeks in Ms. Jefferson's class for me to realize that she would not be pulling me into her neck or asking what was wrong. She treated me like a strange thing. She didn't seem to like children generally but had a certain disdain for the Black and poor ones, for me, maybe because I knew the truth—that she was just like the rest of us. I could never catch her eye in class; she seemed to always be looking just over my head or through me like a window. She seemed to show her teeth when I got an answer wrong. I didn't understand it then but that was the year I began to learn that we come into the world with meaning and that there was history in my skin.

On the day of our presentations, the classroom was a parade of variations on a colonial theme: George Washingtons, Abraham Lincolns, Benjamin Franklins, with construction-paper hats and costume wig pieces taped and glued to little faces. Brown faces, too. Most of the Brown people hiding out in the pages of our textbooks didn't have names—they were the necessary masses being driven off land or chained to it. The chorus, not the main characters. According to our lessons, we hadn't made real contributions, were not yet people. Not like those whose names and pictures and accomplishments made history.

I'd chosen Harriet Tubman. We'd read about her only briefly, a few paragraphs accompanied by a picture of a Black woman holding a lantern. Yet despite the tiny corner of the page given to her in our history book, I knew she was the most important person I'd ever encountered. As I read, the ground had shaken under my feet. Her story lifted off the page and called everything into question—the legality, the morality, the humanity of this history. An inscrutable tension had entered the room when slavery was first discussed. Ms. Jefferson taught it at a distance, as words, dates to remember, hurrying us through the unfortunate time. We didn't talk about what it really meant or draw any meaningful lines between the beliefs of that time and our own. I could tell, though, by the furtive glances and the smirks, by Ms. Jefferson's enforced silence, that that time was not exactly over. It was here now, and somehow I knew that my role was to not press it or feel it or ask anyone else to feel it, but to give everyone reprieve, accept the order, and store slavery as my own personal shame. The only place I had that was my own was my body, so I put as much as I could in my downward gaze.

But at the end of the section on slavery, when we got to those few paragraphs on Harriet Tubman, her story came around and sat me up straight. She had escaped slavery and led scores of others to freedom through channels called the Underground Railroad. The details on the page were so scarce that most of us imagined an actual tunnel dug through the earth connecting to an underground hatch in people's homes. This official textbook story neglected what I sensed was there, that Harriet represented something much more dangerous and holy than the book let on. She was the freedom the forefathers alluded to but were terrified of. She was the true story at the heart of this country, the contradiction and pursuit, the hidden pulse under the war drums, a Black woman in a white man's vision for the world. She broke the spell for me at a time when I was learning what was expected of me. When I was learning to internalize the hatred, the way I'm sure Ms. Jefferson had figured out how to do forty years earlier. Harriet disrupted all notions that I had to accept any of this order as fact. She lived in the shadows and cracks of that world, traversing and widening them until something broke open. If she had found a way to make her body free, I knew that I could, too.

My mom had helped me assemble the outfit. Tied my straightened hair up in her nighttime headscarf, cinched a white sheet at the waist with a belt to make something of a dress. I held her worn-out Sunday Bible in one hand, and across my shoulder slung a tote bag filled with shredded cotton balls. I held a flashlight in the other hand, my lantern. I'd never really enjoyed dressing up. Halloween was always and only the devil's day, according to my grandmother, who found any activity short of praising Jesus inherently sinful. Halloween to her was an open invitation to possession. But as Harriet, I wasn't in costume as much as I was being fortified. At the time you couldn't have told me that I wasn't a superhero. I walked into school proud, defiant, straight-backed. Ms. Jefferson's expression was blank when I showed up to her class, as though she thought that if she stayed very still, the others might not see the resemblance between us. She stood behind the kids, her eyes fixed on me when they asked, "Who are you supposed to be? Are you some kind of slave?" I waited until their giggles died down, and declared that I was Harriet Tubman, that I freed people under their noses. I said it as a dare. Neither the other kids nor Ms. Jefferson said another word. When I gave my report, I talked slowly and met each person's gaze. The shame left my body then. I felt strong, determined, and I could, at least in that moment, see through all that was unacknowledged, unspoken in our class.

. . .

I DON'T THINK HEALING BEGINS where we think it does, in our doing something. I believe it begins in another realm altogether, the realm of dreams and imagination. A realm that I might also call spirit. A place of potential, where possibilities reside, where we retrieve, through prayer or in dreams, visions for ourselves and for the world that make us more whole. And with our visions in place, we can realize them through what follows, our commitment and the steps we take toward them.

I sensed this in Harriet's story, and I listened for her name, catching pieces here and there on how she coded plans for freedom in the spirituals we thought we knew. Harriet, our Moses, who led our people out of bondage. Who could somehow imagine past the barriers, beyond the seemingly immovable logic of her time that celebrated kidnapping and enslavement, and foresee a world where the accepted order of things could finally be exposed as brutal and inhumane.

I don't call on Harriet Tubman here to invoke some trope of a Black woman who must bear the weight of this country's transformation. I am most interested in what I can never know, how she learned to trust her dreaming and how she committed deeply enough to stay the course. The world she was born into was on the brink of civil war and was contained and kept in order by both casual and ritualized public violence, by intimidation, and by the denial of rights. Masses of people were being indoctrinated with propaganda that created and reified the world's most recent invention, race. She led people anyway, through battlegrounds and forests into an iteration of freedom, a new context. How she did so wasn't only a matter of technical or tactical skills.

Harriet Tubman had visions—messages directly divined to her from God.

As a young girl she had refused to detain an enslaved Black boy, and the plantation's overseer hurled a weight at her head, fracturing her skull. For the rest of her life, she experienced pain and pressure to her brain that led to blackouts, visitations, and visions. Dreams in which routes to freedom and warnings of impending danger revealed themselves to her. Premonitions that showed her the future. So persistent and accurate were her visions that despite narrow escapes, and a bounty on her head, and nearly twenty perilous journeys to the South and back to Canada, she was never caught, nor was anyone she freed ever remanded to slavery. She was, in a very real sense, a prophet who found a way to the future, paving a new and unexpected path carved from her commitments and visions.

Some say that in our time of overwhelm and chaos we are at the end of futures, out of resources and hope, that there is nothing left to dream in this reality, that we are trapped on a timeline where we keep remaking disaster movies until we meet our final catastrophe. I think often of the Doomsday Clock that, at the time of this writing, has us at just ninety seconds from the end. The end of time, of human life, brought about by nuclear war or the ravages of climate change or technologies capable of destroying us. Ironically, the clock was created by the Bulletin of the Atomic Scientists, the very group responsible for the atomic bombs that killed many thousands in Japan during World War II in attacks on Hiroshima and Nagasaki. If these physicists didn't doom us themselves, they at least accelerated our downward trajectory, and while they say the clock is a wake-up call to crisis and into action, it feels more like a preemptive seal on our fate, one that generates despair. What would it look like if we refuse their vision of the future altogether? What if there were no clock? What if we were to recalibrate and find a different way?

Lately, our culture has responded to this narrative of imminent extinction by indulging in nostalgias, looking back to some golden era where we imagine ourselves more free and less encumbered with one another and the consequences of our actions. For me, the most compelling nostalgias are precolonial, a time when we honored and sought balance and reciprocity. I string together a vague rendering of these times through stories I've been told, but I know most of what I make of those pasts is embellished by my own imagination, and the challenges we face now remain unaccounted for. Other nostalgias, appealing to some, threaten almost at gunpoint to turn us back and reconfigure ourselves neatly into the hierarchy of the past, submitting to the order of a world that built its greatness on the bodies of others and covered it with the stink of denial. All nostalgias are not equal, but they are all, in a way, a retreat. When we live in the past, we can no longer learn from it. It's this process of learning from our history that is most threatened today, and our failure to do so dooms us to repeat our mistakes. We can look back and recover the lessons, but we can never forget that we are here. That the complexities and messiness of our here and now were sown by our own hands, and we can make something grow, something that is alive precisely because of how it weaves the past and present into a new offering, as beautiful as the most inspired gifts our ancestors left us.

· · ·

IN 2015, I WENT TO Ferguson, Missouri, for a second time during the uprisings. I joined a small group of healers supporting local organizers there who had led the encampment outside the police station since the night after Mike Brown was killed many months before. We set up a kind of pop-up clinic in the basement of St. John and James Church where we did group work and individual sessions. At the top of each morning, an organizer would announce the day: We are at Day 263 of fighting for Mike. It was a marker of time that until then wasn't on any calendar that existed. I was struck that the people we were working with had left behind jobs, graduate programs, family, that they had paused their lives to create and hold open this portal, to make this new time happen. One world had ended the day that Mike lay in the streets and another one was rising from it, taking shape.

The day I left Ferguson, I flew home to Hawai'i, where I had been living for just under a year to be nearer to the family of my partner, Kasha. I spent so much time in the air in those days, touching down in a crisis and then lifting off, landing somewhere new each week. At that time, Native Hawaiian organizers were protecting the mountain Mauna Kea from the construction of the Thirty Meter Telescope that would decimate its summit, and Kasha, my brother, and I had been invited to visit the encampment there. Our friends Loke and Hāwane took us to the top of the mauna and introduced us to her. There, surrounded by clouds, we prayed for her protection. As we finished, Loke turned to me and said, "This is Day 76 of protecting our mauna." As I stood up there on the island chain's highest peak, it was hard for me to see that moment as anything short of spirit at work. Here were two movements, separated by ocean and land, with barely any knowledge of each other, connected through my witness and an invisible, emerging timeline. This, for me, was proof of the possibility to reshape time, to use new markers, to map a way to a new future.

To vision futures is to conjure something that sits outside of your time and circumstance while being firmly rooted in the moment. To listen for the calls of what is not yet here but is waiting just in the wings. The way that Harriet did. Even in the most unsteady and dangerous of times, even now, we need our imaginations, and we need visions.

A few years ago, I read an article about why humans tend to be so bad at predicting the future. What researchers found is that we predict in a linear fashion, but the factor that makes projections most accurate is the ability to anticipate new relationships, unexpected alliances, and possibilities. Visioning is an uncovering of potential. It's revealing what is already there and trying to become, if only we believe in it. When Harriet looked out at her world, she didn't see a predestined set of futures enshrined in law and society. Instead, she factored together the determination of enslaved Africans and the courage of some white abolitionists and through these elements she saw the possibility of an alternate future. Fed up enslaved Black people and abolitionist whites built an unexpected set of relationships and opened a new timeline. What we allow ourselves to imagine, what dreams spring from unlikely relationships, is the beginning of the future.

Visioning is not easy. We are born into other people's visions for us and for the world. From the moment we take our first breaths, we are surrounded by expectations and futures imposed by our families, our communities, and our society: visions about who we will be, what we will do for a living, who we will marry, and how many kids we'll have. Less personal visions shape us just the same: visions about how a society should be constructed, from buildings to borders, to laws and ritual, to concepts of God and nature. We are born into a world populated with others' visions and their own constraints of imagination that still shape how we move, how we feel, who we think we and others are. Just as a fish can't conceive of water, we often don't know about or consent to the visions around us. They become the measure for what is true and what should be. These visions set a path for our lives, opening up channels of possibilities and foreclosing many others. Within their grip, it's difficult to know who we really are or what we might become.

When my fourth-grade self was learning about race in Ms. Jefferson's class, I was really taking on predictions that people have for our lives: projections, visions that become a kind of mandate to maintain the order of our current world. I was told that Black people were less smart before anybody was curious about how I thought and what I had to say. I was told what girls like to do before anybody asked me what I found interesting. I was told whom I was supposed to marry before anybody taught me how to feel and listen to my own body's desire. I was shaped by these visions for who someone like me could be, should be, by visions that crowded out my own feelings and stifled my imagination.

My queerness was always less about being attracted to women and more about a perspective on life, a way of looking at the spaces in between things and always being honest about what I felt. But quickly, into my teenage years, I started to get the message that desire should follow established routes. That I should behave in ways that reinforced the validity of these routes and that I should enjoy it. If I didn't, I should at least have the decency to be quiet. I had learned this message already in the songs I listened to, in the whispers I heard in church about other people around me, both kids and adults. I had somehow thought I'd be exempt from the judgments, but I was wrong. It seemed that everyone was attached to a vision of my life before I could even begin to understand it myself, and any deviation from that vision came with consequences.

The first time I got up the courage to kiss a girl I liked, I was sixteen. We stood there afterward, holding hands, basking in that awkward teenage love, when a police car pulled up. Someone had called the cops on us for kissing. "Your parents know you're out here carrying on?" the officer asked. My parents did not know I was out there carrying on, so I dropped my head and said no. I hadn't anticipated this intrusion. A second earlier I was filled with teenage urges, that soaring rush of hormones and new-love feeling that made the world turn on and show itself to you. Now the color had drained away and my body slammed shut. "Take yourselves home then, and I bet' not see you out here again."

Disoriented and terrified, I complied. I learned the lesson clearly, though: Be careful believing your life can be your own. For some of us, our visions are a threat to order.

THAT WE CAN COME TO BE so completely encapsulated in the world of another's imagination is remarkable to me. If those visions are enforced, they can almost take away our capacity to want something different. I think of the risk it is to stretch beyond the containers that have been created for us. I think about longing. It's a visceral word for me. It's vulnerable and hard to let ourselves desire beyond what we can trust will be fulfilled. Longing is not evidence-based in that way; it's a yearning that comes from our bodies.

There's a difference between wanting and longing. When I was twelve, I wanted Girbaud jeans. Everyone who I thought was cool had a pair. No matter that they were a hundred dollars a pop: Some kids had multiples in maroon, black, and winter white. I wanted them so badly I searched the racks each time I went to the thrift store with my grandmother, looking a size up and a size below. I was willing to negotiate fit for that telling white label across the crotch. I never asked my mother because I didn't need to. I knew a hundred dollars for jeans would be a waste of money we didn't have.

That same year my father ran a booth selling old tools at the town's flea market. On Saturdays and Sundays, I'd roam the market, moving in between the tables of bootleg DVDs and worn-out furniture. One weekend, a new booth opened at the back of the market with what looked like Xerox versions of the brands I knew from school: a Cross Colours hoodie made from fabric that was a little too thin and colors that seemed a little too bright. But hanging up just above me was a shirt that repeated "Girbaud" all the way down in a suspiciously rounded font. I schemed that if I bought this shirt and wore it long, over my JCPenney jeans, someone might read them as Girbaud, too. I handed over my fifteen dollars for the shirt.

The next day, I ironed my jeans crisply down the middle and tested the length of the shirt. Perfect. It was all I thought about that morning in classes: Did people think I was wearing Girbaud? Was everyone recalibrating themselves now that my status had suddenly surged? At lunch, as I was walking by the cool kids' table, one of the boys called out to me, "Hey, is that a *real* Girbaud shirt?" "What? Yeah," I said. "What do you mean?" But the words were just sounds to keep me from dissolving on the lunchroom floor. My plan had backfired. Not only was I not cool, I was fraudulent. I never wore the shirt again.

Want attaches itself to objects we think might make us happy. It fills in gaps we think we have. But longing is something else. It comes from deep inside and is not easily satisfied with things. Often it sits underneath our wants, the thing we desire that we might be most afraid to say. I wanted Girbaud, but really, I longed to feel like I belonged to people. I longed to be seen, loved, and accepted. We can easily accumulate wants when products are advertised to us or when someone around us has something we don't. A commercial tells us that these items will make us happy, secure, or that maybe when we have them, we will finally feel worthy.

Of course, we can have things, we can want them, but that wanting won't be a replacement for this other impulse, longing. That vulnerable, stomach-dropping craving. Longing is personal and, in that way, a part of what might be an authentic self. We tend to long for what our bodies need in order to heal and feel whole.

Visions are rooted in longing.

Years ago, my first somatic therapist sat across from me at the outset of our work together and asked what I longed for, what I yearned to feel or do in the world. I looked at her sideways. I was in my early twenties, working a job I tried to be good at but wasn't, in romantic relationships that never turned out better than my imagination. She was asking me about longing, but it seemed too heavy a word for me. At the time I knew fiending, the craving you get for something that already has you strung out. I knew jonesing, the lustful ache you get for something or someone. To me, both meant that desire could take hold of you and take over your life and was therefore to be avoided. But longing was somehow different, more evocative, yet dangerous in its own way. Longing was a weird, soft, risky word to me. It put you out there. And to be out there meant that you could be shamed or left behind or otherwise made to feel bad for who you were. Longing sought fulfillment. And I wasn't sure fulfillment was for people like me. If your belonging in the world was tenuous because Blackness was a threat, if the cops could be called because you kissed someone, if you could be yelled at in your own neighborhood for wanting ice cream, what use was it to long? And more, what use was it to make that longing known?

First came the answers I thought I should have, that I wanted to be a more effective listener, or to be good at my job, a better worker. I scrambled to think of what was acceptable to long for, but none of it felt true. "But what do you long for?" my therapist asked again, her eyes steady in the face of my squirming. "What makes your stomach jump just to say it?" I paused. It was there, right behind the nausea. I could sense it trying to get my attention.

"I guess, if I'm honest," I said, "I really just want to know how to love."

At a healing retreat earlier in the year, my instructor, Liu Hoi-Man, had said that an obstinate and uncomfortable desire to love and be loved had led her through her own healing journey. Her words had hit me directly in the stomach, called me out. I had felt that, too. I'd gotten swallowed up in the message that I was too Black or too queer, too poor, too fundamentally unlovable, and that belief had started shaping me. In relationships, I was always protecting other people from getting to know me. I kept a safe, disengaged emotional distance, and I got out of there at the first sign of difficulty. I did not really believe that I was worth loving.

"I want to know how to love," I said. "I want to be able to give love, show the love I feel, and I want to let it in when someone says they love me back."

Saying my vision out loud made me feel queasy and small, yet a little more free. And it made me wonder if somehow, maybe in ways I couldn't anticipate, naming it had made it more possible.

I'd known lots of people who didn't vision much. We had learned to stay ready, defended, our lives unfolding as a series of things that just happened to us, never something that we shaped. In grad school, I worked with a client named Saul who came to me for therapy. He had recently gotten out of prison after ten years inside and had found his way into a job at a community organization that provided housing and employment for people with records. It meant a lot to him. He knew exactly the barriers to finding and creating stability after incarceration, the pitfalls and traps, and he knew that his life was hope for others, the proof that they could make it. He came to me because he struggled to focus and was often forgetful at work. During the months of our sessions together, we found that most social interactions caused him to freeze, that there was an almost persistent terror simmering in his body. Some of it, he discovered, was the initial shock of being taken away from his family; a part of him was still suspended, floating over the moment he was arrested. That memory was compounded and entangled with the layered shock of returning, the constant struggle to catch up and keep up and understand what had happened in the time he'd been gone.

When I asked Saul a question about longing, the one I'd been asked by my own therapist, he couldn't find the answers easy either. It was something he'd never thought about for long, or for himself. He'd been focused on surviving each day, not thinking about the future. A lot of his close friends hadn't made it to adulthood, and here he was, inching near forty, living in territory that was completely unknown and unaccounted for.

Trauma can take the capacity for longing, for visioning, from us. By necessity it keeps us shortsighted, tied to the past and focused on tracking and assessing dangers in the here and now. In PTSD research, it is referred to as "a foreshortened sense of future," a hypervigilance that leaves little room for dreams or visions. While the short term, the immediate, can appear to us in vivid detail, the long term, the future, is hazy. When we can't perceive too far ahead, it's impossible to imagine that we can shape what comes and create a future we've never seen.

In the time Saul and I spent together, we thawed some of what was frozen in him, finding layers of rage, regret, grief, and, at his core, a very small boy who needed to feel protected. Before we got there, we named the longing for what his life could be, something that might be a powerful enough conjuring to allow him to feel what had felt too painful or unsafe in the past. "I want to be a vulnerable leader and a present father to my kids," he said. "I want to know that I am worthy and that I can inspire the people I work with to believe in their own worthiness." How would he have known before that this could be true? This statement became the basis for our work together, for every session, and for his future. It guided him from then on, shaping his relationships, his time with his kids, and moved him toward a place he had never before dreamed was possible.

There is a difference between the visions that come out of our most individualistic tendencies and those that arise when we are able to admit that we need other people. I've often found that the visions people articulate for themselves, those that they are most afraid to admit, are their yearnings for connection and their longings to lead and coordinate something that will have a big impact on the world. I've never encountered anyone's most vulnerable visions to be about isolation or money. In rooms where I teach, I ask people to announce their visions. It's a way of showing this point. When we dream from the seat of ourselves, we come into relationship with one another, and have visions for a more reciprocal and balanced world.

The truth is that the visions we inherit, the visions from others that we live inside of, can only re-create the world as it is. Within the constraints of the visions of others, my capacity for love was stunted and Saul was tethered to his past. We need visions within us that make our stomach quiver and cause us to come alive. Then we can show up more authentically, reshape the contours of our community, rework the structures of our world. Harriet dreamed of freedom as a child, long before she was free. In this time, we need the sight that she had to see beyond the walls of other people's visions.

And we need this as our central practice.

• • •

VISIONS ARE A CALL, a conjuring, a glimpse into what can be, but as my grandmother would often say, quoting scripture, faith without works is dead. We name our visions; we say them out loud to bring them into being, and we move them toward fruition by staying the course.

Commitment is the path between your vision and this moment. It is the day-to-day building, practice, and intention that transports you forward to that changed place, whether it's internal or external to you. When Harriet first escaped the plantation in Maryland, she left with her brothers. Scared, they turned around soon after, and she was alone, but committed. She found the North Star in the sky, and she followed it through forests and swamps, freezing temperatures, and hunger to a new and more free life. On later journeys, close calls and the danger of the unknown made some try to turn back, but she insisted that they stay the course. Her dedication is almost hard to fathom, but she never lost a passenger on her train because of her commitment. At times, she dealt with harsh conditions, narrow escapes, but there's something about the unanticipated that allows commitment to activate. When we set out with a vision, it crashes into backlash, barriers, fear. Commitment is what gets us through the middle of change, when the outcome seems bleak, when it seems we're lost or can't go any further. Commitment expects our despair but doesn't waver. It comes from inside of us, keeping steady when we lose hope, or give up, or decide to step away. What lives inside us does not go anywhere, but waits, so we can return to it. Commitment to the North Star, our vision, brings us through. To what and to whom are you committed? What do you long for? And what is worth traveling through the unknown to reach?

Our ability to dream of something different, to name longing, to articulate a vision and commit to it, directly correlates to the likelihood that we will experience it, that it will be realized. It's the way we bring about change for ourselves, and for the world. When we are besieged by visions that do not match our longing, some of which are sinister, it's unlikely that we'll stumble into freedom. Freedom is in the gaps, in the nascent and emergent, in the unexamined space between things—but it is there. We can call it down. We call it down when we listen to our dreams. When we let the unconscious and the imaginal show us the way around what it is we see right now. We call it down when our present can be in conversation with what could be. In prayer or meditation, in what we ritualize, our visions become more real the more space we give to them. There are already visions around you that have shaped most everything about our world. If they do not serve us, perhaps it is time to revisit our imaginations, perhaps it is time to dream new dreams.

Underneath our current reality is a future waiting to be conjured.

2

HEAL

Not everything that is faced can be changed, but nothing can be changed until it is faced.
—James Baldwin, "As Much Truth as One Can Bear"

I WORKED FOR A LITTLE WHILE WITH A MOTHER WHOSE SON had been killed in an encounter with police. In the years that followed, she'd been brought into political organizations working against violence, asked to tell and retell her story. She had become a tireless activist, attending meetings and leading marches. It gave meaning to what she'd been through, a way to act when it seemed like life itself had betrayed her. But she'd begun to fray. The same people who had brought her in now found her hard to be around, testy, rigid. Her productivity had become the perfect place to hide the worst of her pain. Whenever I heard stories of brutal loss like hers or saw mothers and fathers and girlfriends stand and speak at press conferences, I always wondered who held them that night, or the next, when the wave of grief came. Who listened when they were messy, or when their story was incoherent? Without that kind of support, I knew that trauma could metastasize into a way of being.

Initially, the mother was reluctant to see me. The first time she sat down, her eyes fixed on my face, she pointed a finger and said, "It's not that I don't think I need this. It's that if I really get into this, I know I'll fall apart. And there'll be no coming back together." My stomach dropped. I didn't have any answers or promises that working together would ease her loss, or that allowing herself to feel and processing what she felt would create any immediate relief, but I did know that if she didn't do something—that is, if she wasn't given the space to not do anything but just be—the grip of her pain would only get tighter. Over time, she opened up to me and I stayed close as she shared, turned my body toward her as she described the unthinkable. Through the years, I've learned that, more than anything, presence is a kind of permission for honesty. My work is not to imagine that I can bear the weight that someone else holds but a commitment to not look away. I was there, ready to bear witness to the wave of her grief, a reminder, I hoped, that there was life for her still on the shore.

Recently, I was speaking on a panel about the state of social justice movements in California. It was a room full of political strategists and veteran community organizers, and I was doing my best to make a case to them for why healing and personal transformation are necessary for social change. At the end of the talk, during the question-and-answer session, an older man stepped to the mic and said, "We can't heal our way out of fascism or climate change. We've got more important things to do." A few people let out uncomfortable laughs, presumably in agreement, and everyone turned to look at our panel at the front of the room. A part of me deflated. I'd used my ten minutes trying to present what I thought would be well received, the science of trauma and healing, redefining both in ways that expanded their reach, from their impact on the individual and the collective to the importance of embodied healing, but I knew it was a hard pitch for a room that didn't take feeling as seriously as they took what they saw as political threat.

There was a time when I had felt the same way. That in order to be serious about social change, I couldn't feel. That I had to hide even from myself what haunted me. Never mind getting support to heal or even telling anyone what troubled me. I soon learned that everything that mattered was happening outside of me, that my only focus should be the meetings I went to and how many doors I knocked on. But it got to a point where no amount of making myself useful could quiet what I felt inside.

I decided to go to therapy.

This was around 2006, long before there was a public conversation about Black mental health, when there was still so much stigma against getting support. Every Tuesday at 1:45 P.M., as I walked to my appointment, my mom would call like clockwork for her daily check-in. And every time she called, I would tell her I was on my way to therapy, and she'd ask with worry, "What's wrong?!" "Nothing specific," I would say. "Remember? I go every week." To her, and likely others of her generation, therapy was reserved for emergencies, for breaking points, for when numbing or distraction was no longer enough to get you through the day. The kind that looked back or looked in, dredging up what you had been convinced was yours to endure, was never a voluntary undertaking. It was assumed to do more harm than good.

Somewhere around that same time, I sat down to dinner with a friend of mine, a seasoned political organizer, and shared that I'd been increasingly interested in understanding trauma. I confessed that I'd started weekly and, up to that point, secret therapy sessions that were helping me understand places where the past had taken hold of me and not let go. That I thought knowing what was possible in the human mind and body added new dimensions to political work. That I could feel there was something in this that we needed to know to organize well, to care for one another. My friend rolled her eyes and sat back in her chair. "Are you becoming one of *those* people?" she said. "Soft and always talking about your feelings?" Tears rushed the back of my eyes, but I held them in. It crushed me, this message that healing was not for us. What was I ultimately fighting for if not a world where I could sometimes be soft?

What I offered in response to the man at the podium that night, what I was too hurt and confused to say to my friend years before, is what I'll offer to you now: Healing and social change are not, in fact, unrelated. To pry them apart is to exacerbate the issue. They are inextricably linked, braided together, interdependent processes of transformation. To ask if we can heal at the same time that we engage social change is, to me, like asking if we can love at the same time we make change, if we can make music or eat food. How could our personal development ever truly be at odds with social transformation? How could it happen without it? And yet, this was the way so many of us thought. How did we get here?

In other moments of Black freedom movements, the spiritual, cultural, and emotional elements of our lives were held by institutions that tended to our development as well as our connection with the transcendent. Churches were one such place, and before that the African traditions brought with us in the belly of ships shaped us similarly. At different times since then, Black people have been punished, as have Indigenous people, for practicing their spiritualities. More recently, many of our churches seem to have gone wayward, preoccupied more with appearance and wealth than the interior development of their people. As congregations have left in droves, an unforeseen casualty is the understanding that our internal worlds, our flourishing as people, have bearing on the material worlds we inhabit and create.

Healing, or care, is still essential for guiding the how of what we build, the visions for the world, and is the principle for how we navigate the challenges therein. When we commit to social change, we remember that systems can perpetuate and create harm, or they can foster healing and resilience. This is especially important to know because we can mean well, be committed, have a vision for change that inspires, but if we are not actively and intentionally attending to our own healing or practicing a healing ethic, we unnecessarily limit what it is that we can do.

Most of the time, we come to the work of making the world anew because of the pain this one has caused. Our wounds can give us the initial surge to fight back, though this energy is fueled by our most frightened, defended, and adrenalized selves. Ultimately, it's not sustainable. The wound grows even as we use it, eating away at the person who holds it, acidifying all we do. Every place of contact or relationship bears potential pain, and our strategy can become too protective, rather than tapping into the prospective. We are most powerful when sourcing our energy from possibility, from our visions, not from the pain we know, but from the world just outside of what we can now see. Our energy is most potent when we make room for our grief and anger, when we allow ourselves to feel, and our direction becomes clearer.

Over the years, my work has shown me a curious pattern: When social movements and social change organizations face significant external political pressure and backlash, it can turn inward, and they can fracture along the lines of individual and collective unaddressed traumas. They break apart in places where we are replicating patterns that harm others and ourselves. We cannot ignore our wounds, nor can we work over or through them, nor mine them for energy. Instead, it's through an orientation toward healing and repair for ourselves and others that we recover our capacity for feeling, for relationship, and, with that, the ability to strengthen our bonds and work together. Then we can create and lean in to visions for ourselves and a world beyond our fear. As we attempt to reconfigure the world where it has been unjust and where our systems and beliefs have hurt us, so must we transform ourselves, our values, our cultures, our actions, and our spirits.

The grief that poured out of the mother I spoke with that day was heartbreaking, world-shaking, and it deserved space and witness. If we were to feel our pain out in the open, name it, step into the ceremony of it, and let the knowledge guide our steps, how might that change every single thing we do? How might it change the world?

"TRAUMA" IS A WORD WITH its own fraught history that I use simply because it helps me to understand cause and effect,

how injuries happen to the human spirit, and how we twist
and wind a life around our wounds. Native psychologists like
Eduardo Duran have developed the term "soul wounds" to expand our understanding of trauma into spiritual and historical
realms. And psychiatrist and Harvard Medical School clinical
professor Judith Herman and her work on trauma have helped
me to understand the political history of the field itself. In her
groundbreaking book *Trauma and Recovery,* Herman shows that
our growing understanding of trauma has always been tied to
political frameworks. When Sigmund Freud began studying
so-called hysteria in women as part of the anticlerical political movement of late-nineteenth-century France, he found an
epidemic of childhood sexual abuse. He halted and hid this research because it was too inflammatory and potentially disrup-
tive to powerful men's lives. Later, research into the trauma of
veterans during the two world wars was more concerned with
how quickly soldiers could be returned intact to the front lines
than with the true depth and nature of their pain. It was only
through anti-war movements led by veterans in the 1960s and
their campaign to investigate the traumatic impacts of com-
bat, and through feminist movements in the 1970s and '80s
insisting on unearthing the hidden stories of abuse that women
had buried, many since childhood, that trauma as the field we
now know began to take shape. Because of these movements
we began to understand more about post-traumatic stress: that
survivors of domestic abuse can carry the same symptoms as
veterans of war, that disabled veterans, women and children,
are human and their pain matters and will impact their lives
and the lives of their loved ones.

We are still shaping how trauma is understood: whose stories are included and whose harm is recognized. Racial jus-

tice movements in the last decade have started to talk openly about the trauma of poverty and of oppression, expanding this knowledge and recognizing its far-reaching effects. The mother I worked with taught me something that I had often felt but hadn't seen before in any textbook: that Black bodies carry the weight of generations of trauma while continuing to experience traumas every day, and that too often we hold it silently. What has happened to us and our ancestors—the legacy of enslavement, Jim Crow, lynchings, segregation and desegregation, mass incarceration, and the onslaught of crack—is still here in the air and still here in our tissues, and despite what we might think or how we've been trained, that matters.

Trauma researcher and author Bessel van der Kolk has highlighted how trauma, originally thought of as a psychological phenomenon, is in fact physiological, experienced in and throughout the body. When we encounter a threat, whether assault, neglect, or ridicule, our bodies want to save our lives and mobilize our varied resources—from the dispersal of hormones to the readying of our muscles—so that we can take the necessary and appropriate action. This uptick in energy and the activation of our survival strategies are ancestral genius at play. Over the development of life on earth, our microbial, animal, and human ancestors faced a great number of threats and learned, in fortunate moments, how to elude death, destruction, and isolation from their communities. These lessons were then encoded in their brains and throughout the rest of their bodies and passed down to us, making it easy for us to respond to threats quickly without too much thinking and to relay critical information from our bodies to our brains and vice versa.

These necessary responses are a part of our everyday interactions with one another and our environment. However,
when what we face overwhelms our ability to respond and/or
to escape unscathed, or when we are given the message to
suppress the body's reactions, our nervous systems don't know
that the traumatic experience has ended, and our survival
response continues to exist in our bodies. We live then in a
near-constant state of reaction, either scanning for an indication that the threat has returned or reproducing aspects of
the experience in our relationships and lives in what many
understand to be an attempt to complete the threat we feel.
It is alive in our tissues, our muscles, our thoughts, and our
moods. It lives on in our behavioral patterns, our habits, what
we do and don't do, what we say and what we are afraid to say.
I explain to my clients that trauma can arrest a part of you,
that you can have a region of your body living out of time,
out of step, with the rest of you. That a physiological memory
from ten or twenty years earlier can be lodged in the structure
of your fasciae, and therefore in your actions and relationships. This is what we mean when we say that trauma stays,
that it lingers long past its welcome in our bodies.

When we don't attend to trauma, it can start to permeate our lives. While we may know that the initial pain can
hold our bodies hostage, we often overlook that it refuses
to stay within the confines of our singular bodies, that it
moves through relationships, within our families, our communities, and across society, multiplying the pain. Intergenerational trauma can pass down, sometimes epigenetically, by
our inherited genes, and most clearly through the ways our
families interact. How are boundaries set? Are people humili-

ated or threatened? What gets talked about, and what goes unsaid? How is love shown, and to whom?

Complex trauma, first introduced by Judith Herman, reveals that trauma, once thought of as a single catastrophic event, can be a repetitive or ongoing accumulation of threats to our survival, such as neglect or emotional or physical abuse, leaving the body on constant alert.

I know much of this from my own childhood. My parents were both, in their own ways, beautiful. Intensely loving and love starved. Our home was both warm and, to me, randomly volatile. The fear was there every day, even if the violence wasn't. I knew love in the nuzzle of my dad's beard and in the warmth and softness of my mother. But their fights were unpredictable and sometimes violent, so I learned about vigilance and dissociation, how to be here one moment and gone the next. It wasn't safe to be out in the open.

In my first memory of life, I am four or maybe five, in the bedroom that I share with my sister. The slatted doors open to our living room, and on the other side of them is a storm. My father is a dark cloud descending on my mother, lightning bolts and thunderous growls, and she is falling. Her dress flaps open and I see bruises, deep purples and blues. At some point a beer bottle is broken and from the way it amplifies the horror in my recollection, it is broken over her. My sister, who is probably twelve years old, must have pulled me away because I'm no longer standing there, I'm facing another wall and she is holding me. We are an island in this storm. If we can hold each other through, we may survive. It is not our bodies that we are protecting but something much more core and unnameable. I don't remember and neither does she if we are shaking or crying or still, but it is terror that is coursing through me, and everything in me, barely even formed, is already shattered.

For a long time, this memory was a part of a montage of frightening moments I recalled, moments where the world showed me something I didn't yet know was possible. That the people you loved the most could be caught in a violent tangle. For years, this scene replayed in my mind, not only in moments of fear but, surprisingly, also in moments of intimacy. Your mother, your safe harbor, could be hurt, and your father who tickled and hugged you, with those same hands, could abuse. It was shocking, being catapulted to a dangerous place and trying to understand: Can I be safe in this new world?

Later, during my training as a therapist and somatic practitioner, I consciously learned what my body had already known. That trauma breaks apart our ability to experience safety, belonging, and dignity. That these needs are core to our ability to develop as human beings, grow, create, engage with others and the world, and express and protect ourselves. Safety is the capacity to feel free from threat, which includes the threat of hunger and neglect. When we feel safe, our nervous systems can quiet, allowing for other capacities like imagination and expression to come forward. Belonging, similarly, is our ability to feel that we are a part of something, of a community and the world around us. Trauma can make belonging contingent or dangerous, leading us to seek isolation or supremacy—both strategies to break belonging. Dignity is the capacity to feel the inherent value simply in the fact that we exist. It is the seat of agency, of choice. When we can witness and tolerate dignity in others, we build a foundation for collaboration, for co-creation, and repair. When dignity breaks apart, a space opens up where shame comes in, telling us stories of our inherent worthlessness.

Even when our conditions change, we can still struggle internally to feel or believe that these capacities are possible for us: We may never feel safe even though we have what we need; we may question belonging even when we are clearly wanted; we may live with a persistent shame that doesn't allow for boundaries or choices that care for us. It's the fracturing of these capacities that follows us through our lives.

When I was a child, my nervous system learned to constantly search for threat even when there was none. A pervasive shame held me together, mediating at all times who I could be to belong. I was somehow at fault for the abuse, at fault for my mother's unhappiness. I was fundamentally bad. I was also left with a belief that belonging was innately dangerous—better to hide my own needs so deep that they would be almost imperceptible even to me. I carried this embodied trauma forward into all my relationships, hiding from the possibility of connection.

TO HEAR MY FATHER TELL IT, my grandfather was the best dad in the world. He was superhuman: a military man, a skilled tradesman, and a ladies' man, too. My dad had only a few stories he told, and they were of his father's accomplishments, not about any adventures they went on or lessons he learned firsthand. I asked my mother about it one day, why there was such a gap between my grandfather the myth and the man, why there was hardly anything in those stories that gave me a feel for his voice or his way. I must have sensed somehow that my father couldn't withstand this line of questioning. The story my mother knew and had heard from my grandmother was that my dad never saw his father. That he was abandoned by him. My grandfather was known to call and promise my young dad a visit and then leave him waiting all day on the steps with a backpack of his most precious things. This image broke my heart. And I could see in it how a child who longed for a father who never came would need to break with parts of reality, would still need, as a man, what he had missed as a child, to be the center of someone's world, to be loved. My dad always maintained the story of a perfect father because that imagined father could somehow follow through on his promises.

To that imagined father, my dad was lovable.

My dad didn't know that his father had likely been in his own pain that siphoned off his supply of love, nor did he know that his own childhood hurt was the basis for his violence and rage. That his trauma rippled down to us.

In my sixteenth year, I was sexually assaulted twice, both times by boys I considered my friends. I know very clearly that none of it was my fault, but I also know that I had gotten accustomed to having my body too close to the fire, to the rage of my father. I befriended boys with tempers that I tried to quell, who took more than they gave, because it was familiar to me. I had learned to seek connection at the expense of my bodily safety, to lose my own limits in order to belong. Eventually, transgression became familiar, a fact of relationship. I learned to quiet my body's responses, a wince, the desire to pull away. I could numb my own indicators that I'd had enough. The abuse my father acted out on us was a predictor and a preparation for other violations.

Trauma spreads and transmits beyond our individual bodies. We are social, interdependent beings, communicating almost constantly with one another about how safe we are, how threatening, how willing we are to connect, and how likely we are to leave. So when our past invades our present, as is the way with trauma, we inhabit our current relationships according to the concerns, fears, pain from another time. When we talk of intergenerational trauma, this is a part of what we mean. It can be passed down in those earliest and most intimate relationships. My dad's unresolved pain from his own childhood, and the trauma of his father that preceded him, became a feature, an organizing principle, of my relationship with him, and it warped itself into a trauma that lived on in me.

PAIN IS TRANSMITTED ACROSS A power grid. It's sent to the places where we don't fear the consequences of it spilling over onto the people less powerful than us, onto seemingly less deserving bodies. It shows up as abuse toward a partner who has fewer means to leave or in the scapegoating of whole communities for our suffering.

My father grew up a well-known, academically gifted, and charming football player in a small Texas town. Outside of the context of Southern racism, born in another time, he might have seemed destined for the kind of fame or power given to his white counterparts with similar attributes. But, as they say, to be Black means that you have to be twice as good and most of the time even that isn't enough. The pain and frustration my father felt were palpable in the home, the deep internal breaks of missing his own father who never showed up, but also the broken promises of this country to Black men. He felt he deserved a different future, as a man, and if he had a bad day at work, was laid off, or otherwise felt the blunt end of racism, it wasn't his boss who suffered the rage of his dehumanization, it was us—his family, those who had less power and recourse than he did, my mother first and then the children.

Sending pain down the ladders of power, illuminated in the work of writer Sonya Renee Taylor, somehow reinforces the hierarchy itself, cementing the belief that some are deserving of violence. While my mother could pass some of her pain on to me, on the whole we were all left to internalize it and make believe that we had earned it. To think otherwise was a threat to order. The dance of patriarchy, racism, and aching poverty trapped my dad in this cycle. As far as he could see, he would always be scrambling for resources, yet always feel responsible to provide. He was told that having feelings was feminine, that he couldn't feel the sadness, despair, longing of his child self and stay a man. Against this backdrop, rage made him into someone, contoured him against love, reinforced, even though it was fleeting, that he could be powerful in this world.

Oppression is the distribution and concentration of trauma into bodies and communities designated less powerful. It is the mechanism that leaves these same bodies and communities without the resources in time, money, or support to heal. Of course, that's not to say that trauma doesn't touch every kind of person. It can and does. It just means that the frequency and force will likely be different. For some, trauma is inflicted by institutions that restrict rights or incarcerate disproportionately, as well as inflicted within their homes. They feel it in the constant stress of underemployment, in bouts of hunger. Some will have more to inherit from what history has handed down. And some will not have the capacity to address the part of it they hold.

Whether we thought about it this way or not, my mom and my sister, my brother, and I were suddenly connected to a web of other mothers, partners, and children who had experienced abuse and carried that trauma with us. And we all were part of a Black experience mediated by the trauma of oppression—a threat to our collective safety, belonging, and dignity. It undermines safety by threatening our bodies and narrowing our resources. It withholds belonging in laws and disparate treatment and assaults dignity wherever mythologies of supremacy persist. Such complex and compounded trauma undermines the very idea of community, conveying the notion that it is too dangerous to be together. We can fracture or internalize messages of inferiority to stay safe. These traumas weigh on Black people and communities and, unprocessed, they accumulate and intensify. Together, we have not had a moment of reprieve to grieve what has happened and what has been lost. And we have not at large scale possessed the resources we need to restore our safety, belonging, and dignity.

Every person who has experienced trauma interacts with every other person's trauma. It is a tangle that impacts everything we do. Our struggles extend into our families, friendships, and communities, into our places of work and worship, our organizations, and each person's trauma becomes entwined and interconnected with everyone else's. Even when we see this matrix of pain and intend to relieve it, what already lives in us undermines what we are able to do. Is it any wonder that the changes we try to bring to our communities, to the world, the things we try to build, sometimes splinter?

MANY SOCIAL JUSTICE MOVEMENTS, whether stated explicitly or not, are, in part, an effort to heal. People are drawn to them, looking for an end to the same unfair treatment and perpetual trauma experienced in their personal lives. It was a part of what pulled me in. I felt for the first time that what I experienced growing up wasn't something to hide; it was important information about the world as it is. And it seemed like the only place where that firsthand knowledge was taken seriously. Even if there wasn't space there to process or feel it, there were solutions being offered, ways to prevent or at least interrupt other similar occurrences. And, in a way, that's one of the powers of social movements: We are bringing to them what matters most to us. In this way, they can be places for our deep healing, but if we are unconscious of what we are doing and why, they can just as easily become places that trigger our trauma and further separate safety, belonging, and dignity. If it is our pain that fuels us more than our visions, we can't last.

I have seen the lingering impacts of trauma in people's personal lives show up elsewhere in their organizations and institutions, fracturing the foundation of collaboration and undermining our ability to do powerful things. I've seen leaders so afraid to trust that they move in secrecy or try too hard to hold on to control. They struggle to build strong, connected teams. I've seen others so terrified of belonging that they frustrate or sabotage the work with their constant suspicion. And there are those who use overwork as a way not to feel, and who expect others to do the same. A brilliant leader I once worked with flew into a rage and flung a chair across a room when given some necessary but hard feedback. The vestiges of childhood trauma broke through, undermining my colleague's ability to stay calm, causing them to put others down, to protect themselves, no matter the harmful fallout. Months of building trust and connection, hundreds of hours of late nights and missed family time, exploded in that one moment as the chair went across the room. It was devastating for everyone.

Whoever we are, we pour our stuff into our work. We bring our habits, our coping mechanisms, behaviors, and patterns to whatever it is we do, and that becomes the basis of the cultures we build. When we focus on external change without tending to internal transformation, we act out the worst of ourselves in the places where it matters most. We are left in a reactive state. We answer the moment based on past scripts and experiences rooted in our bodies, and we throw out short-term, shortsighted, narrow-minded reactions instead of the long-term, collaborative, transformative solutions we need to bring positive change to the world.

THE MASSIVE SCOPE AND SCALE of trauma with its intertwined and compounding paths could easily overwhelm us. What's the point of looking closely at something that is everywhere? But by viewing trauma as a teaching tool and a frame for understanding individual distress and social challenges, we can learn from it. It shows us what is too much for a human body to bear before breaking, what it takes to disarm our defenses, which societal structures increase despair, and how we might

organize ourselves as a society to optimize individual and collective well-being. This way of examining trauma tells us what
it takes to really heal.

For a long time, I searched for a definition of healing.
Most times, what I came across in the world of psychology
was the treatment of symptoms, not the root cause, or healing as defined by the ability to get back in the saddle and become a more productive citizen. In other circles, healing was
an escape, a disengagement from life, high-end retreats and
self-care classes where you could pay to temporarily keep the
messy problems of the outside world at bay. Most of the time,
we define terms according to our context, so it's not surprising
that our terms for healing reflect the destructive individualistic and productivity-oriented tendencies of our society. In my
own work, I needed a definition that pointed me in a direction, but that kept me firmly on the ground, that helped me
understand what the full scope of healing could be.

I've been working for years now with this: Healing is the
process, often lifelong, of restoring and reawakening the capacities for safety, belonging, and dignity on the other side of
trauma.

It's a simple definition but it works for me. We can't heal
or act effectively under active threat, when our safety is not
assured. We either find safety or create it with who and what
we have. Belonging is about bringing us back into the world
around us, and back into relationships with others. Dignity
is where we feel our worthiness again, where we are about
the business of eradicating shame and expressing our agency
and choicefulness. These principles can bring us to a path
of our own growth. And I think these principles have social
implications. Most of the time mainstream healing and well-

ness put the pressure on the individual to "heal" when really it's about fitting into a society that may itself be the source of the trauma. How can we best practice a culture that restores these capacities and build societies with these principles at the center?

I recently became a parent. The intimacy that my child came ready for awakened in me some of the places where I was still metabolizing my past. If you've never looked into the eyes of a baby, if you've never let them take you in, study your face and movements, I suggest this dose of presence. One of the first times my child looked at me that way, I felt myself recoil, afraid of such an intimate connection, a body memory from my own childhood. The shame story followed that wondered if I were good enough to be looked at by her, my child. I felt it happen inside me, a slow-motion retreat, a preoccupation with my own worthiness, and I caught it, adjusted, breathed, and chose to find my way back to her, to meet her in presence, to witness her curiosity, and let myself be witnessed. Just that simple move interrupted the beginning of a transmission of disconnection to my child. That particular trauma, at least in that moment, did not successfully root itself into our relationship and did not stretch into our future.

Healing happens in moments as simple and profound as this, when we are able to tolerate, feel, and express something in our relationships that before was out of our reach. It reinstates our abilities to choose something other than what our fear dictates. It will not make us perpetually nice or necessarily peaceful, but it will help to make our responses correlate with what is happening now. Healing, I often say, helps us fight in the places we need to, but love in the places we long to.

Healing is not an acclimation to unjust conditions. It isn't about quieting down or fitting neatly inside what already exists. This brings me to "resilience," a related word and one I tried for a long time to avoid. Even as I write it now, I can hear the groans from people I know: "Not this word again. I'm tired of being resilient. I want to thrive." I feel it, but there are a few reasons why I think it's important. Around 2019, I cofounded a collective called Resilient Strategies. We wanted to understand trauma and how resilience strengthened our organizational cultures. We found that resilience isn't a label someone can give you. Black people, in particular, have been told how resilient we are for surviving some of the worst kinds of abuse. But survival does not necessarily ensure resilience. One of our elders, Alta Starr, would say that instead of thinking about resilience as the way we cope after trauma, we should think of it as our birthright, how we come into this world. To be resilient is to be engaged, creative, adaptive, and relational. It's to remember that you are a part of this world. It is the opposite of isolation and habitual protection. We find it in dance at the moment we sync up with the beat or when we witness someone else finding in themselves the doorway to the ecstatic. It's there in what we call nature when we can feel as if we belong to that larger system. It's in everything that rightsizes you, brings you into reverence and presence, where you leave your control or hiding place, and suddenly you can create within the world, and be taken aback in awe of it, too. Resilience is found in the most transformative of healing journeys.

Healing is not a place you can arrive to. And whatever you call it, it is the ongoing work of enlivening our interiors, waking up our souls. Healing is an orientation to living rather than a destination. It is a commitment to mending and developing our emotional awareness and integrity.

The basis for freedom, for power, is a body where we can be alive and changing, to become people who can relate to one another and the world around us. Our emotional selves are not inconsequential to liberation; they are foundational.

Healing is not an easy process. The things that suffocate us and haunt us are persistent and pervasive. Between a rock and a hard place is no place to live. It's true that there are real limitations to what healing we can do internally and relationally without also changing the pressures that we each face every day. Still, the limits don't mean that we neglect healing altogether, or that we pretend it isn't worthwhile. It's not lost on me that some of us would rather stay in the realm of healing and never face the terrifying and massive questions of how we live more justly in this world together. Others would rather stay focused on justice than come home to face whatever unresolved tension or pain they carry.

We commit to our own healing in part because the realization of what we are dreaming of rests on it. It is our responsibility to one another to do our internal work, not so that we feel good alone but to stay an active part of the whole and to refuse to pass down to the next generation what pain we've accrued. Healing ourselves is not the end of the line but brings us into relationship with others, and allows us to do the work that brings healing to the wider world. For society and movements, it could mean that safety, belonging, and dignity become our metrics for the well-being of our organizations and the people inside them. We could make room for authentic connection, timely repair, and intentionally build more trust and transparency. We might study the resilient and life-giving aspects of our cultures and practice while being aware of what drains and depletes. We could be careful about how we bring in the most traumatized of us, making sure we scaffold them with care. We could use how we gather together not to numb ourselves from the pain we face, but to build a collective resilience that carries us over the long term. And we could source our work with our visions, not our pain. *How* we work is as important as the work we do. Some years back, I told myself that I wouldn't follow anyone whose vision for the future didn't show up in their day-to-day life in how they cared for themselves and the people around them. Being open to healing makes a leader open for learning and is the basis of a kind of compassion that encourages others to step into the unknown of transformation.

When we can heal our trauma, our lives deepen as we widen our capacity to experience more, to perceive more, and to connect more. As we start to feel safe with one another and feel like we belong together, we can relax into appreciating the fullness of life and our place in this ecosystem. And we can bring our transformed and transforming selves to the necessary work of building a better society for everyone. What do we choose to build then? Who or what would our systems protect? What would it do to movements, to our society and culture, to have the principles of healing at the very center? And what does it do to have healing at the center of every structure and everything we create?

I think about this often for my family. What if, in another world, survival had not been the order of the day? What if my father had been held as a boy whenever he needed it, or if he'd been asked about his pain? What if my mother had been talked to sweetly so often as a child that she expected the same treatment in every adult relationship and had known how to leave when it was absent? What if a community had surrounded her after she'd been hurt, loved her abundantly, and nursed every wound? What if both my parents had been given options and outlets, if their own family members had sought to repair what they had broken in them? What if the love we felt for one another had been expressed generously, with no sense of scarcity or fear? Or my sister and I had embraced before feeling terror and not because of it? I know that time does not turn back. But what if, I wonder, we were to do it all now? Can healing reach through the weeks, and months, and years, and free us? I believe something comes back to us when we listen to and hold one another and when we take time to learn ourselves and tend to what we find. Through healing we can change both the past and the future.

FEELING AND THE BODY

I touch my own skin, and it tells me that before there was any harm, there was miracle.

—ADRIENNE MAREE BROWN,
Pleasure Activism: The Politics of Feeling Good

SOMETIME AROUND THE AGE OF TWENTY-SEVEN, I RELEARNED how to cry. I'd hardly ever seen anyone in my family cry. My mom I'd seen fewer times than I could count on one hand and my dad I'd caught only once, when walking by a door cracked open. Every kid where I'm from knew that crying was not tolerated. "Stop crying before I give you something to cry about!" On cue to that refrain you learned how to suck the air back into your chest and swallow the emotion whole. You fixed your face so as not to show any signs of fear or pain. I never knew why exactly it was so enraging to see us be small or fearful, to see how we really felt. But I learned the lesson so well that even as an adult, when my eyes welled up, I unconsciously absorbed the tears back in. I covered over the feeling of sadness or fear so quickly it was almost like it was never there.

One day, my therapist noticed this trick during a session. "What does stopping yourself from crying take care of for you?" she asked. "I don't know," I said. "I guess I'm putting myself back together because I think I'll get hurt if I feel upset." "Mm-hmm," she said and scribbled in her notepad. "And what's the cost," she asked, looking up, "of stopping the tears?" I thought about it and got that uncomfortable feeling you get when something you pride yourself on shows you that it's really a coping mechanism of a scared child. "Well," I said, "I don't think I really get to know how hurt I am, and I just end up holding on to it." There it was. It all connected, and I realized what I'd been doing.

Of course, if you had asked me if crying was healthy, I likely would have told you it was. But just after that session, in the car, the sadness I felt from realizing how much I'd not allowed myself to feel hit me, and almost as soon as the tears started to form, they dried up, just as they always did. Knowing that I was suppressing my tears wasn't enough to allow them to come. Around that time, I was hanging out with a group of friends talking about playlists of our favorite sad songs, breakup songs, or songs that could make us want to cry just from the first chord. I got the idea then to compile the saddest playlist I could imagine and take myself and my songs on a date, a crying date. I booked a private hot tub for an hour one night that week. With headphones on, I repeated, "I'm safe enough to feel what needs to come." I lay back in the warm water. Twenty minutes in, Sade started singing "King of Sorrow," and I started to cry. Immediately, I felt the impulse to suppress the tremor but instead relaxed the muscles in my face and chest, and took a deep breath, allowing the waves to pass through me. The cry dropped past my diaphragm abruptly and into my belly and came out in a convulsive, shoulder-shaking sob. I was flooded with memories of crying, being immediately told not to, and the dull ache of those same cries that, it turns out, had been there all along, waiting for an opportunity to release. I sobbed all the way through Leonard Cohen, Donny Hathaway, and the whole rest of the playlist. In the end, I was spent, my body somehow more surrendered to gravity, but somehow emotionally lighter than I'd ever been. I had retaught my body how to cry.

For at least the next year, I'd book a cry date whenever I felt myself get backed up—a heaviness in my body was my sign that there might be something I was holding. Later in the hot tub, I'd be surprised that a sideways comment a friend had made a week or two before or a moment of loneliness I'd felt would be lodged right there in my chest. Eventually I learned to sense the urge to cry, and even if in the moment it wouldn't release, I could lure it out later, safe under a pile of blankets with my headphones on.

For healing to take place, for it to be felt, for it to root, remake, and rearrange us, it has to happen not only in the realm of our thinking, but in the soil of our bodies. Healing has to be embodied. When I teach courses on embodiment, this is where I begin: inviting us to become reacquainted with our bodies that are undeniably near, yet these days can seem so faraway and unfamiliar. Embodiment is, not so secretly, the principle at the center of this book. For years, we have tried to outsmart our bodies, override them, and ignore them. That feeling my clients have had of late, an uneasiness, a discordant tone I feel in myself, too, is an indicator that our best intentions and even our best politics have not created in us the kind of change we long for and need. We know somewhere in ourselves what is fractured in us and our world and that the necessary redirection of our species will not be achieved by a change in just our thinking or only through our smartest ideas. It won't be a performative change either. Instead, this change that we are called toward requires something of us that is radical and relational, cellular and generational, that brings us closer to one another and is measured in the very feeling of our lives.

The word "embodiment" is used in a couple of different ways. It can refer to what it is that we've learned to do, the skills and habits, the ways of being, that live in us, that we've *embodied* over time. Brushing your teeth doesn't require you to think it through each day because you've practiced it so frequently, but neither would your tendencies to people-please if that's one of the lessons you've picked up over the years. Behaviors become automatic with enough repetition. Embodiment can also be used to describe our developing awareness of ourselves, our emotions and habits, and our ability to perceive sensations throughout our bodies. The more we can act from both our thinking and our feeling, grounded in our own felt sense, the more we might say that we are *embodied*. Here are some principles that guide me and that I'll discuss at greater length during the chapter:

• What we practice, what we do over time, can eventually become automatic; that is, it no longer requires our thinking to execute. We just do it. Something is truly learned when it is embodied (whether it's riding a bicycle or having the capacity to trust someone). What we embody may be aligned or misaligned with our values or may be helpful or harmful to us as we learn and embody practices both consciously and unconsciously over time.

• We can build our awareness of what it is we do automatically, how we do it, and how it came to be—which gives us the possibility to change.

• We can increase our ability to feel our emotions rather than deny them and allow ourselves to feel what we deeply long for in ourselves and the world.

• To transform and become who we intend to be more often, we have to practice being who we are becoming.

These principles go against a lot of what most of us are taught about healing and change. We've been told that once we identify what's wrong with us, we can fix it, and trade out one behavior for another. But knowing something alone does not produce changed behavior, and when we try to impose new ideas on a body that has its own logic and cares, they won't last. When we approach our healing this way, we further separate the worlds of our thinking and feeling, and our failures open up a space where shame can live. It's a setup. When we rely so heavily on our thinking as the sole basis for healing, we miss the resource, the wisdom, and the reality of our bodies.

OUR SOCIETY TEACHES US THAT thinking is our most elevated function, our minds are the seat of rationality, and our thoughts are, therefore, impartial and trustworthy guides—much more reliable than the unpredictable, sensual animals that are our bodies. In the West, many of these ideas can be traced back to the roots of the Scientific Revolution. Francis Bacon, the British philosopher, forwarded the notion that relentless experimentation on the natural world is the basis for the knowledge of how things work. Physicist Fritjof Capra, in his book *The Turning Point,* describes Bacon's approach to science this way: "The terms in which Bacon advocated his new empirical method of investigation were not only passionate but often outright vicious. Nature, in his view, had to be 'hounded in her wanderings,' 'bound into service,' and made a 'slave.' . . . Bacon's work thus represents an outstanding example of the influence of patriarchal attitudes on scientific thought."

Philosopher René Descartes introduced the concept of mind-body dualism, his theory that the mind and body are distinct and mostly independent entities. For better or worse, the thrust of his work gets reduced in the mainstream to his most memeable phrase: I think, therefore I am.

Both Bacon and Descartes contributed to the mechanistic view of life that came into greater influence later through the work of Isaac Newton, an English physicist and mathematician, and that left an indelible impact on how we view and live our own lives. This foundational idea that anything in nature could be understood by taking it apart and that dissection and isolation could reveal the hidden logic behind everything propelled us forward scientifically, allowing us to classify the world, but it disappeared and diminished the role of relationship and context and our ability to see the connection between all living beings.

If we were to look forensically for when we started to split ourselves into mind and body and to look at the world and one another as machines that could endlessly work, this is one such catalytic moment in time. Humans decided to conquer nature, no longer living as a part of it, or attuned to it, but becoming the masters of it. Just as the mind was split from the body, we were split from feeling, and ranked according to our association with the untamed world. Nature, womanness, the Black enslaved, and the Brown masses were all "bound in service" to a still-forming identity and class of the white and monied—who were in thrall to the advances of science and the seemingly endless reach of patriarchal intellect.

Such a view of our own bodies and the natural world converts us all easily into objects when we relate to one another. If we treat our bodies like machines, as if they are only containers for our thinking, then our emotions, in their unpredictability, become the wild in need of conquering, too. And it would follow that if we do not feel or if our society views feeling as a failure, our culture might lose its grasp on what is truly humane.

When we stifle our emotions by thinking that they're too messy or inconvenient; when we measure our body's value by its thinness and productivity; when we feel that we or people we know are undesirable or disposable because they are disabled; when we see the nonhuman natural world only as raw material for products to be consumed without end or renewal, we are operating inside a paradigm that dehumanizes and objectifies. So many people I've worked with have come to me because they can no longer get their bodies to do the things they want them to. Some want bodies that almost robotically perform life's tasks rather than considering what their bodies might know, what they are trying to say, or understanding their bodies' limits. Our bodies are much more than the fleshy vehicles for our brains, much more than objects for another's desire, much more than cogs in a wheel.

. . .

SOME YEARS BACK, I DID a podcast interview and the host asked when I first knew that I had a body. I hadn't thought about the question before and I couldn't provide a precise moment when I remembered waking up to my body, only times when it came more clearly into view through a capacity or limitation, or through feeling. It is hard to know you have a body in those early years of life, when you are so much a part of the collective, your family or community, that your own body can be hard to distinguish from the whole. But your own body is nevertheless there, recording, reacting, relating, expressing. One of my first recollections of bodies was being told that a body was something to cover up. So in one way, my body was first outlined to me according to which parts needed to be hidden. Later, when I crashed into a tree stump and flew over my bike's handlebars, my body radiated with a global pain. And when I got older and my sexuality came on, my body was a furnace, fueled by a persistent new desire to merge with other bodies. My body was also connection.

When I was in the fifth grade, my godmother died. She was, as I remember, one of those people who warms you without trying, whose laugh falls down on you, whose face was always obscured behind the billows of Newports. When she got sick, our house filled up with waiting, all holding our breath until my mother got the call and made the announcement that she was gone. The first loss of someone whose imprint I could still feel. I missed her immediately in the only ways I could as a child, as one less place to feel safe, one less adult hand on my back when I needed it.

That same year a classmate's brother killed himself during the World Series. I had met him once the previous year at my classmate's birthday party. It was the first party I'd gone to in a wealthy or white home. The parents had turned the basement into a club for kids, with a shimmering disco ball hovering over the center of the room. I was excited to dance that night and surprise them all with my moves, but I never got to it. Walking into the party room, I was struck almost immediately with strobe-light-induced vertigo. Somebody caught me falling and my classmate's mother took me upstairs to wait on the couch for my mother to retrieve me. The brother came then, perhaps assigned, perhaps not, to sit with me. Whatever the reason, he spoke to me, asked questions, seemed curious. I got the sense that he, like me, had a sadness that distracted him, that made him less concerned than the other boys with hiding his softness. When he died the next year, I replayed what was left of our conversation, two awkward children speaking across different but related chasms, without the words for what was in us. I lived long enough to find a name for mine and eventually to find a way, through my body, to some relief. But he didn't.

For about a month following the passing of my godmother and the boy, each night before bed I would play Michael Jackson's "Will You Be There" from the *Free Willy* soundtrack I had purchased on cassette. Stomping, clapping, dancing. I spoke to my godmother in the dance and the tender boy who had sat next to me on the couch. I spoke to loss itself. I asked God every question in my dance, what happened to them, what would happen to me, what was happening around me, and why didn't I have control. I spoke through my body to the nothingness, letting it devour me and birth me again. My body discovered new ways to move, and new meaning in the moves I already knew, a new/old language. Each night my dancing before bed was a ritual until the night when I didn't need it anymore, until I had digested the grief and accepted it as a part of me. I didn't realize it at the time, but this was the moment I discovered what my body knew how to do, and the moment I decided to live in it.

Everything that happens happens in our bodies. Everything we feel, say, think, risk, every connection we ever have is experienced there. Our bodies are the expression and container of our lives. The tissues and muscles that can hold on to a trauma can also learn a dance, can live out a vision, can pick up a habit, can grow and age. It's through our bodies that we experience and engage life, and it's in our bodies that we heal.

Our minds were once thought of as a creation solely of our brains, but recently psychiatrist and UCLA professor Dan Siegel defined them as an "embodied and relational, emergent self-organizing process that regulates the flow of energy and information both within us and between and among us." The mind is not just a function of our brains but a co-ordinated mapping that includes the information perceived and recorded by other parts of our bodies. Our best thinking happens as a full-bodied experience, because no matter how much we try to separate the brain from the body, it is irritatingly located there, inside of it, a part of the ecosystem that is us. There is a reality that our bodies connect us to. They grow, age, and eventually die. Our bodies join us with the cycles and laws of continual change that are true for all life. We protect and connect; we both expend energy and require rest. And our bodies are somehow a collection of living stories, too, of where we've been and where we come from, a profound record of our ancestors' survival. An individual body, through its language, rhythms, needs, connects us to the body of our species, to the body of life around us, and to the great movement of life across time. Our bodies are made of this world, organized and pulsing stardust, and yet they each hold something precious and distinct that is uniquely us. Our bodies are the proof that we are alive and that we are here.

Miraculously, too, our bodies feel. They respond to the world with emotion, the physiological sensations that happen when we encounter stimuli, both external and internal. We lose someone we love and are taken over with grief. Someone jumps out at us from around the corner and our bodies respond with fear. These emotions are involuntary, and they are universal in the sense that we all experience them. Feeling is the conscious allowance of emotions, letting them run through us so that we digest them and understand the messages they offer. When we deny this process and stop up feeling, like I stopped my tears, we are treating ourselves the way we might machines, and we lose the human opportunity feeling gives us to learn and grow. To deny the life of our emotions and the process of feeling is to deny how alive we are and how inseparably bound up we are with one another.

Many years ago, I fell onto the path of somatics, which would eventually become the foundation of my work. The definition I was first given of somatics is that it is the study and practice of how change happens in bodies. The root word of somatics, "soma," translates from Greek to "the body in its wholeness." By this we mean the body in its physical sense but also as the place where we feel, where we sense, where we make meaning, and where we engage with the world.

I see somatics now also as the study of our bodies, trauma, and the practices we generate to develop awareness of our bodies and transform them. I think of embodiment as related, but inclusive of all the practices, rituals, and ceremonies that people have used across time to transform not only individual bodies but our collective bodies as well. The ceremonies, dances, and songs that every Indigenous culture around the world has created for birthing, for death, and for grief, to prepare for battle and the changing of seasons. The rituals that give people in community space to heal and express, and where we sync our bodies with one another's and feel the presence of what we share that lies beyond words.

My first somatics training was in 2010 through Generative Somatics, an organization in the Bay Area whose mission was to train social change leaders in trauma and equip them with somatic practice in order to build more powerful social justice organizations. I was working as a fundraiser with one of the groups selected for the program. During the first session, I spent that initial hour of introductions terrified that I would show unexpected emotion in front of my co-workers. I steeled myself, tightening my body, and paid attention to not take too much in or, worse, let too much out. First, we worked on centering, a practice meant, in essence, to ground us. We started with scanning our bodies for sensations that the teachers described as the very language of the body, that the body was always expressing and responding. I noticed how challenging it was to locate my sensations. I was tracking so much outside of me. The breathing of the person next to me, the roaming eyes of the teacher. Next, they instructed us to soften the contractions in our muscles where, they explained, shame and trauma could lurk. We could take our bodies back from these experiences, reinhabit the places we'd abandoned. One of the teachers, Vassi, asked that we feel the edges of our

skin, to breathe through our pores. It was a strange instruction. I had just started therapy, and I was still a long way from
being comfortable with anything too abstract. I tried it anyway. I took a breath, exhaled. I immediately noticed how tight
my ribs felt, like there was a rubber band around their base,
how short and shallow my breath was as a result. The teachers
encouraged us then to soften and expand the muscles in our
chests, to make more room around our hearts, they said. I'd
never considered the muscles in my chest at all, but I could
feel that my chest was contracted, caved in, exactly around
my heart. How long had it been like that? From the strength
of the contraction, I could tell it was longer than just that day.
It felt familiar, comfortable, and well practiced, even though
I hadn't known it just the moment before. I was suddenly in a
new conversation with my body. What else was in there?

Everywhere I carried my attention I could feel the quiver-
ing of a muscle that wanted permission to let go, or another
that resisted, tightening even more under my curiosity. I tried
to "breathe through my pores," as instructed, and suddenly
understood how far inside myself I had retreated. I couldn't
feel my skin at all. My whole body was bracing. In my mind's
eye, I saw an image of a tiny version of myself living behind a
door deep in my chest, like one of those figures that emerges
on the hour from a clock face. This was the control center of
my life. For the first time, I realized that this was how I always
felt. Here I kept myself tightly guarded and hidden, protecting
what was most vulnerable from coming out and being hurt.
The more I breathed deeply, the more the bracing threatened
to give way, to what I had no idea. I glanced around to see if
anyone else was feeling the way I was or if they could see me
feeling. Had anyone else just had the volume on their sensa-

tions cranked up? My body was trying to tell me secrets that I hadn't known how to listen to before. I looked up and saw the teachers at the front of the room, noticing the subtle ways their own bodies shuddered and shifted with each instruction. They were releasing and rearranging. They were feeling. It seemed so simple and natural to watch them do it, but my body would not surrender; the tightness wouldn't let go.

SOMETHING CHANGED FOR ME THAT DAY. I had started on a journey of discovering myself not as I tried to be, or pretended to be, but as I was. I learned that the places where my muscles tightened were contractions, which, in somatics, are seen as protective or reactive impulses that remain in the tissues. An unprocessed shock might show up in a contraction around the eyes, a constant startle. For me, a contracted chest was an impulse to contain myself, to stay small and hidden. Across our bodies, our muscles can tighten, pulling us in to protect or keeping us pushed out and defended against the world. These places can become anesthetized over time. Many clients I've worked with have had long-standing contractions in their chests, as I did, or in their jaws, their stomachs, or their shoulders, but their bodies no longer register the pain it takes to hold the contraction. The muscles and fasciae around them adapt, and the body fossilizes this protective imprint. It's a remarkable example of how the body can learn and embody what it has practiced. If we don't feel the fear or threat has ended, we hold on to the posture and, hidden within us, it can sabotage our lives.

Unprocessed trauma or conditioning by our families or social expectations can cause our protective body to become

our predominant way of meeting not only potentially traumatic moments, but any moment in which we perceive stress,
even when there's no real threat to our lives or bodily integrity.
Our protective selves can show up when we get into a disagreement, when we are so afraid that we might be hurt like
we once were, and our bodies can automatically go into an
embedded fight stance as we find ourselves trying to injure
another person with our words because we are afraid of injury.
Or the stress of being loved, even as we've always longed for,
can activate an automatic retreat. We might disconnect from
the source of the love, afraid that we aren't deserving or ready
yet to meet it. Our bodies don't interpret the value of the
stress, good or bad, but if we assess something as stressful it
can elicit these responses.

When our reactive selves become the primary part of us
that meets the daily stress of our lives, we put ourselves at a
disadvantage, though we don't realize it. Our protective bodies
are made of quick actions that are helpful in life-threatening
situations. They search for and identify danger and choose
an immediate action based on what is perceived. But when
overused they intercept our ability to be in this moment. The
more we perceive the world as threatening, the more our reactivity will take hold of us, convincing us that it alone knows
how to take care of us. But our reactions always answer to a
memory. To the past as it visits our relationships and our lives
in the present. What we need to feel, process, or learn now
will be lost in our attempt to defend or protect.

Reactivity is the mechanism of time travel that I discussed in the last chapter, taking us, though not consciously,
out of this time. The more we are jolted into reactivity, the
more we lose our grounding in the present moment as we

respond to the vestiges of the past. This loss of presence is a loss of agency. If we are always caught up in responding to the conditions of another time, we are not able to respond as thoughtfully to the conditions of this one. My own reactivity protected me from past hurt, but it left me guarded even when what surrounded me was the acceptance I craved. I couldn't even perceive that love could be there, let alone open myself up to it.

Constant or frequent reactivity is unmooring. We are more susceptible to knee-jerk reactions, perceiving threat over opportunity, and, ungrounded, we become vulnerable to the certainty espoused by others, the certainty of the person who hypes our fear, perhaps of the dictator or pundit who uses our insecurity, tells us what to do with it, names our enemy, and instructs us in what we must do to protect ourselves.

There is real danger in this moment, mounting political and ecological threats. But our ability to respond in grounded ways is warped by our culture's hyperreactivity. The constant barrage of news intentionally activates our fear, perhaps because it is created from the fear of someone else, and the drum of social media sounds a relentless warning, fueled, on the whole, by our most reactive and addictive capacities. We live in a state of outrage that sparks and fades but never permeates our systems quite deeply enough to really change us or call us into sustained and meaningful action. Instead, our bodies are left defensive and often depleted. Whenever we receive information, the way we meet it and with which one of our bodies shapes what we are able to do with it. The question then is through what process can we soothe our reactions and allow ourselves to meet the challenges of this moment in full-bodied presence.

• • •

THAT FIRST DAY IN A somatics class, standing there so afraid to feel, I saw suddenly how I lived in an almost constant state of reactivity and fear. How my body was holding protective contractions that kept my ability to feel my current emotions at bay. As surprising as it was to discover all the effort my body was making to armor me against threat, it hinted at the possibility that there was some other way, a yet unfamiliar but perhaps more expansive way of being in my body. I began to see that this possibility came through the act of feeling.

It's hard at times to explain what it is that happens when we feel. It isn't exactly logical or linear. In some ways, the best explanation is spiritual for how softening the muscles in your chest can change how you breathe, the way you think, the things you say, the way your life feels. I worked with a practitioner who would wrap me up in a blanket and squeeze tight so that the muscles in my chest could finally release, trusting that I was still protected. Still armored. The emotions and memories embedded in those muscles rushed forward and out. As unorthodox as it might sound as a therapeutic approach, my tolerance for intimacy deepened almost immediately when those contractions started to loosen. I could stay vulnerable with another person longer before feeling the urge to protect myself and withdraw. The connections I began to make with the people I worked with qualitatively changed. Somehow with a softening chest, there was more room to listen to the concerns of my clients without rushing in to fix or know, less need to defend or assert myself, and much more empathy and compassion I could offer.

When I work with clients, my job is not to tell them what they feel or what they should be feeling, but to create enough safety so they can surrender into letting their bodies feel. Most people need the explanation that our bodies already know what they need to do and how. It's a kind of permission to allow what might feel or look weird or wild to come out. Our bodies know somewhere how to cry, how to tremble through fear; they know how to buck off big feelings when they need to; they know how to sink into an embrace.

One woman I worked with, a high achiever who was sexually abused as a child, was unable to feel empathy for others because she hadn't ever been able to tolerate the feeling of her own helplessness. After a few months of sessions, she allowed herself to be held by me as she sat, shaking, under the table, reliving that early fear. This time, instead of having to stifle what was there, she was able to feel what had gotten stuck inside, a frustration with her caretakers, the deep-rooted feeling that she had once been small and had needed an adult to really see her. As these emotions ran through her, she could also begin to feel the resources she had around her now, my companionship in the fear, and the love of her husband, who had supported her healing journey. Feeling allowed something inside her to integrate, and the self-compassion she was able to generate changed how she worked and her relationships with the people around her. To feel an emotion is to allow it and let it run through, to learn from what it is telling you about you, about your relationships. Feeling is a self-acceptance of your own emotions and the wisdom of your body. It is the root of the work I do with most of my clients.

Make your question a quest. My therapist says this to me when I don't know how to describe exactly what it is I feel. I know this means that I am holding on too tight for control. A significant part of feeling is not allowing ourselves to fall too quickly into naming or categorizing what we feel, but to allow and witness. Simply asking what an area of the body might say if it were held, or placing, consensually, a hand to support a place where someone feels a holding or contraction, most always elicits stories and more sensations. It can be tricky, though. Just as our avoidance of feeling can become our normal, we can try to live in emotions, or rather perpetually revisit them. Sometimes we can get stuck in a way of emoting, or focusing on emoting as evidence of feeling, and that can be its own means of hiding or avoiding another feeling buried even further underground. Authentic feeling is not performed nor is it summoned. Feeling is allowed. It is emergent. It is a listening that aligns us with our real indicators. Feeling grounds us. It is proof that we are alive.

Numbing is one way that we protect ourselves from feeling something we are afraid to or are under-resourced to feel. Or that we may not have the support or time to feel. We numb with all the coping strategies we know: work, alcohol, drugs, sex, food, social media, and any other activity humans do that can be made into distraction or an eject button to leave our bodies. Numbing is an important option for us. Sometimes blunting or leaving our sensations is the best temporary solution. Sometimes alternative transcendent experiences, where we leave our sensations on purpose to join in another realm of consciousness, can offer us the opportunity to retrieve something we might not otherwise have had access to. Feeling itself needn't turn into an obsession or another kind of supremacy. It is offered as a counterbalance to a worldview that denies its wisdom.

It takes resource to feel. But what we think of as resource

can be expansive. Human and animal relationships often provide resource for us to face what was previously unfaceable. If we are open to it, trees can help us feel; their steady strength can be an ally, a way to ease our fear. Feeling needs resource and gives us resource in return. Feeling is where nuance can emerge, where multiple and, sometimes, contradictory impulses can make sense inside of us. Where we can resist clamping down too quickly on who we are, what we think we have to believe, and let what is true to us reveal us to ourselves. Reactivity and the binaries of threat and safety limit what it is we are able to dream and experience in our lives. In our bodies, in feeling, are experiences not yet felt, sensations not yet known, and solutions we have not yet imagined.

Feeling is revolutionary, a disruption to the status quo. Though it feels personal and happens in our bodies, it doesn't need to be a solitary action. Feeling and connection bring us into the world and into relationship with one another. Some things seem too big to be felt alone because they are. They require the collective to hold the space for big feeling, for it to move through, and to remind us that we're not alone. It's not practical to imagine that we can feel the weight of historical trauma as one person. This is why we meet in the streets. As much as mass protests and direct action are about putting strategic pressure on opposition, they are often a gathering space for our grief and pain because they are too big to feel alone. Protests don't get reported on this way, as an eruption of collective grief; on the news they are riots, and we begin the cycle of minimizing the feelings that bring people to the streets, and ultimately we miss the message. We need those spaces and others, too, where our grief can swell, where feeling for feeling's sake can reconstitute us, where our empathy for one another can build. A community, a society, becomes one, remains one, I think, through sharing feeling.

Somatics as a field of study appealed to me because it was a path to reanimating our bodies, reclaiming ourselves. It spoke to something in me as a Black person who had been taught in any number of ways that my own body was human-adjacent at best. That our culture, our dances, and our worship were uncivilized. I felt alive with my people, but it didn't seem that our aliveness held value in the world, and sometimes even with us.

But somatics has its own limitations. Its halls are decorated with brilliant teachers who have not always escaped the conditioning of their times. It has often borrowed from cultures while holding to the supremacy of its own. It has, until very recently, through the works of Resmaa Menakem and others, had very little to say about culture and even less about what Brown bodies might already know, even when it has silently taken and repackaged the teachings and philosophies of Eastern martial arts or African dance. Somatics, in a way, is born from the original fracture that separates us all into feeling and non-feeling, wild and civilized. It's a solution to a problem created when the mind was given supremacy. Nevertheless, it's a necessary inquiry, a beautiful invitation to learn what our bodies know about healing and about social change.

Studying somatics awakened in me the proposition that I might not need to tame my body. And if my body was wise, then maybe the bodies I come from were wise, too, especially in the ways we moved with one another, in song, how we could catch the spirit and become possessed with the very essence of God. Maybe there was wisdom in how I'd seen us lay hands on one another's electrified bodies in church. There was a style, a reverence, and, yes, a rhythm that we'd refused to relinquish. And I started to wonder, as I studied somatics, if maybe it was exactly that, those elements of culture, that had gotten us through the worst of it.

In the last several years, the question of ritual as embodiment, as healing, has called me. In my own culture, I could sense and feel remnants of previous traditions that have carried across time. There are mostly gaps, though, where we might have once had a ritual for birth, death, marriage. Rituals move us as a collective through these transitions. I can feel what we've lost. Ancestor Malidoma Patrice Somé once said, "We need ritual because it is an expression of the fact that we recognize the difficulty of creating a different and special kind of community. A community that doesn't have a ritual cannot exist." As much as our individual rituals for healing open us up to connection, our collective practices, what we share, move constrictions out of our cultures and usher in change. Rituals are the churches without walls, the antidote to our denial. Feeling together can both bring us together and free us.

Our society has gone through too many traumas while commanding that we deny our grief and our compassion. Our feeling of it all. Our processing of it and getting to the other side, bringing our new insight into ourselves along with us. I wonder at times if the trope of the dumb American could be understood as the unfeeling and reactive American, if the supposed stupidity is actually the consequence of emotional denial that, at this stage, has become feverish, delusional, antisocial. I wonder if the distinction matters. Mostly, I wonder if a value of feeling that interrupts that perpetual denial might create the opportunity to come down from the confusion of reactivity into the complexity, beauty, and challenge of taking on board and sitting with what has really taken place in our country and what can be done about it.

Somewhere along the way we were taught to stop feeling instead of being taught to stop what harms us, as though the feeling were our enemy, as though the feeling were hurting us. To move forward and address the harm, we have to feel.

As Audre Lorde said in her essay "Poetry Is Not a Luxury," "The white fathers told us: I think, therefore I am. The Black mother within each of us—the poet—whispers in our dreams: I feel, therefore I can be free."

REMAPPING RELATIONSHIPS

It is not those differences between us that are separating us. It is rather our refusal to recognize those differences, and to examine the distortions which result from our misnaming them and their effects upon human behavior and expectation.

—AUDRE LORDE,
"Age, Race, Class, and Sex:
Women Redefining Difference" in *Sister Outsider*

"YOU SEE THAT LINE ON THE GROUND? FOLLOW IT TO THE END and make everybody move around you." These were the instructions of my sister's best friend in high school. Her name was Carole and she'd come to live with us because she was white and pregnant with the child of her Black boyfriend. That combination of offenses caused her parents to kick her out and us to take her in. We were at the mall, and she had noticed my meandering path through the crowds. I was bumped and smashed trying to make my way back to my family, and my ten-year-old body had started to brace and cower through the aisles. "I've noticed," she said, "that if I don't back down, men will eventually move out of my way, so they don't crash into me. They just expect that I'm going to move, and I don't. Try it."

I had doubts. Carole was older, taller, whiter than me, but on her encouragement, I set a path through Dillard's to experiment. What I noticed first was how surprised people were, how they would jump at the last minute and look down, perplexed, at this unrelenting Black child. I focused on the line, on where I was going, my body staying filled out even when I could feel the heat of the person coming closer. I didn't seek collision, but I didn't avoid it either. Only once did I crash into a couple who did not or could not see me. It was startling to us both but their confused "Oh, I'm sorry!" was an unexpected reward. I was suddenly affirmed as someone whose body existed and mattered. And their confusion was the upending of a silent agreement. Mine had been the kind of body that made way, that yielded, politely invisible, that apologized for not contorting quickly enough. Theirs were the kinds of bodies that moved unencumbered toward the sale rack. Now both they and I were unsure of who we were to one another, and that gave me more room somehow to breathe. Each time I tried it, I'd come back sheepishly smiling, amazed at how it worked and how I felt about myself on the other side. Carole nodded. "See," she'd said. "They know you're there. Don't give up your space."

It was one of my first lessons on presence and focus. That a sense of embodied conviction and self-possession was an unspoken communication and could move people from my path. It was also a lesson in social contracts, in how choreographed our relationships are to one another, what we come to expect from the bodies around us, whose body gets to remain intact in this world, and whose must bend. It's hard to appreciate to what degree history shapes our relationships to one another. It's hard to notice how it can invade each moment through the habits and conditioning we've come to embody. How it can contour who we care for and our ability to really see one another. History was never the story of great men alone, as our textbooks would have us believe. It was always the story of relationships. Theirs and ours. Of how we related to the world around us and how we related to one another. The stories we told about who our people were in relationship to God and to the land. The stories of encounter with the unknown other. The ways we enshrined these stories and our identities in our culture and practice and in our bodies. The origins may feel distant to us now, but we inherit beliefs and patterns of relationship by watching how the people around us move. Who is listened to and seen, who is adored. Who is invisible. Who is lifted up. Who is hunted down. We learn in this way who we are, and who we have been, in relationship to the world's other inhabitants.

When I remember my ancestors, for whom disagreement or self-defense was enough reason for violence to come down on their bodies, I think about their wherewithal to teach emotional survival strategies to the generations that followed, to have them perceive danger first and mask their genuine responses in certain company. I imagine the white people who codified their own emotional comfort, if not in laws, then in cultural norms, and, either explicitly or implicitly, accepted the violence done on their behalf. I think about how that emotional entitlement was passed on to the following generations by example and instruction. It's some of what I felt navigating through the crowd at the mall. And I think about all of that when I drive up to the gas pump ahead of a car I didn't see coming in, and the driver slips the word "nigger" out the window in disgust as she drives by. There is history in her behavior the same as there is history in my anger and my silencing of it.

This social contract, this order, makes sense by being so ubiquitous. Yet it still can be changed. If we are unaware that we inherit these relational models, we end up re-creating some version, some derivative of the relational dynamics we have witnessed. It is easy for each of us to replicate what is embodied around us, historical impositions of another time mapped in our bodies, telling us who and where we are. And yet, though it's hard, it is possible to live with the lessons of the past, to face history without becoming its instrument. When we look to the nature of our relationships with one another, we can become more skillful and authentic in our interactions, and see that there are ways of relating that might allow us to connect and come out of the automatic past and entrenched ways of being so that we can meet one another now. Not bypassing our history but moving forward in its knowledge. Our ability to do this is key—our relationships, our social connections, are the bridge between individual and societal transformation.

In the summer of 2015, I attended a somatics training at the dojo of one of my teachers, the aikido master Richard Strozzi-Heckler, in Petaluma, California, just north of San Francisco. I'd flown directly there from the first Movement for Black Lives Convening in Cleveland, where thousands of Black people from across the country, representing many different organizations, had gathered to learn and strategize together about the emerging movement to end police violence.

We all wanted to be on the same page as we moved forward. I had led the community safety team for the first three days of the event, where all of us were trying to protect attendees, staving off constant attacks from disrupters, police, and counterprotesters. So when I arrived at the workshop, I was shaky, spent, and reeling from how a loving gathering of people could be treated as a threat.

Later, while I was receiving somatic bodywork, a practitioner gently massaged the contractions held in my face, in my forehead, around my eyes and cheekbones, insinuating to my fasciae that there was more space to relax into. As the tension eased and my body began to let go of the holding, my eyes started to move in and out of focus. Memories flashed: my father's face, me staring down at my feet in class, the deferential smile I'd laid across my face as the police liaison at the Convening. I realized, lying there, that something in my gaze was learned, that downcast way I met the world. It was inherited. I hardly knew anyone in my family who couldn't soften the focus of their gaze to escape. It was a trick we had developed to stay safe, though it was not our natural posture. As I felt the tension leave my face, it became clear that the first ancestor of mine who had made the decision to soften their gaze and drop their head had done so under duress, under threat, had constructed a mask. They had made a decision for the sake of their own survival, to ensure that their line could continue. They had taught the mask to us. And both in that gesture of survival and encased at the core of that decision, I suddenly knew that there had also been a prayer. A prayer that their posture, their dulled eyes, might be undone at some point, by some generation later. That there might be a future time when a descendant, when I, could relate to the world from an uncompromised body with brightened eyes, when I would have the space to be unguarded.

I was reminded of Maya Angelou's poem "The Mask," in which she shows the social and emotional regulation of Black people as a demand of the time and their endurance of it as a way of loving us now, a gift passed down from our ancestors.

They laugh to conceal their crying,
They shuffle through their dreams
They stepped 'n fetched a country
And wrote the blues in screams.
I understand their meaning,
It could and did derive
From living on the edge of death
They kept my race alive
By wearing the mask! Ha! Ha! Ha! Ha! Ha!

Emotions become enslaved whenever bodies are oppressed. For our ancestors, certain emotions and expressions of those emotions were forbidden in public because they might give rise to an energy willing and capable of opposing injustice. To violate that unwritten order was to risk more violence. And so very often those feelings of rage, of grief, of pain, simmered and burned inside. Stifled and masked, they became tethered to their oppressor's contentment, tethered to a forced sense of societal order that created an illusion of safety, bound in an unjust, precarious, and inequitable relationship. One that made it necessary for Black people to smile and reassure that they were satisfied with and grateful for their lot in life. And to never scream their pain.

There was a danger in expressing emotion, too, because of

what it might do to those training to be the oppressor. Hearing the familiar and heartrending cry of a human in pain could threaten to interrupt the project of making socially acceptable that which was inhumane. Closing off their ears and hearts to such a sound meant learning to extinguish their empathy, to teach a narrow compassion to their children, and to find a tenuous, anxious safety in pretending the human they hurt was a monster. Empathy, mutuality, and connection are dangerous to injustice. They can unravel what is otherwise a fragile, imposed order. For safety reasons, then, we are all taught to push our emotions down and away rather than feel them. If we felt, imagine what we might change.

This is where my downward gaze came from. The one I carried with me in interactions with strangers and in my relationships with other people. While these are not the same times that our ancestors were born into, they are dangerous and retaliatory still, and I am grateful to know how in some moments to use my mask, to leave safely and undetected, with my assessments, my emotions, and my body folded out of harm's way. There can be consequences for lifted, clear eyes, for undeterred bodies, for asking for what you deserve. I'm not always prepared for those consequences.

We all have our ways of interacting with the world, our masks, passed down our lineages, and when we know how and why the mask came to be, we know it is not the true shape of our faces. That knowing is how we remember when it is time and when it is possible to put the mask down. Everything changes when our emotions are freed from the dictates of history, when we can relate in an undefended way and find a path to one another.

Moving out from under the weight of our histories is not

easy when our relationships have become a conduit for the beliefs and stories and enactment of oppression. Often, we have learned to see one another not as tender, striving, fallible, or real but through projections and assigned roles, through whatever lens the world has taught us to read one another's bodies. We have learned to stop listening to the sound of our own desire or heartbeat; we have stopped trusting our internal voice.

Real relationships are made of feeling. They are an exchange in which we are open to one another's ideas, emotions, and perspectives. Our avoidance of vulnerability and discomfort, of the hard work of relationship, is the root of the isolation many of us feel—and this isolation prevents transformation on any scale. Healing always happens through relationship, whether it is relationship with a therapist, a tree, or a grandmother.

Each of us in this country is related, many by blood, though we struggle to admit it or to wrestle with what that means not just in politics but to our bodies. We are also related to people in countries we've never visited, by blood, through the air we breathe, through our labor, through the waters. Across this earth are our kin. What we do shapes the lives of others. We exist in an impossibly complex web of relationship.

We spring from and never really escape these skeins of interrelatedness that weave beneath every lie we tell of separation. Lies we tell of some inherent difference between us we call race, about ranking and taxonomy of human beings based on skin color and tone, gender, culture, religion, ability, and class. The lie is not that variation exists, but that variation can be organized into worthiness. These lies we tell create division instead of connection. We tear apart our fabric of relationship and deny one another instead of using our connection to build what we all need. Relationships are our interface and could be our remembering. They are most alive when they are chosen, shaped, made, not according to who we should be or are trying to be but according to who we are. They have the potential, if we free them, to be the place where we can risk encountering one another and being encountered, where we can create a new pathway of connection and experience together.

Our only way out of these inherited scripts, which threaten to cleave us so soundly from the reality of our relatedness, which threaten our demise, is to remap our relationships and redefine the contours of engagement. But to do so, we need skills that trauma or oppression attempts to take from us. Skills of connection and collaboration. Skills of authenticity, boundaries, and trust. Authenticity so that we can come to know the self who lies underneath our conditioning. Boundaries to help us learn to navigate our changing needs and maintain love and connection. Trust so that we can do things together, build, play, and create.

AUTHENTICITY

BEHIND THE MASK IS WHO we are. In an exploration of relationship, we start with authenticity because being oneself is the foundation for connection. It's impossible to really have relationship or be in relationship with others if we don't allow ourselves to be there in the first place. But this begs the question: Who are we, really? Recently, while teaching a somatics course with a group of young Black organizers, I was explaining authenticity, what it meant to be centered in oneself, present, open, and connected. A young man raised his hand and asked if being authentic meant being a "real one." I thought about how we use that phrase as Black people, how to be a real one means to be honest, thorough, to be ourselves despite the pressures, consistent, true to what we feel, steady. "Yes," I said, "being authentic means that we're real." It's as simple—and complex—as that.

By this definition, authenticity isn't a personality trait that people simply possess. It is a way we decide to be, how we choose to interact with the world. It's a willingness and, I suppose, an ability to both be oneself and be in the discovery of who that really is. We are not being authentic when we pretend to be smarter, nicer, or meaner than we are. Instead, we are authentic when we can sometimes say "I don't know," when we can confess that we don't want to do something that might please someone else, or when we can admit we're hurt or afraid. Our authentic selves aren't perfected or performed. Nor do they usually show up in social media posts with just so lighting and curated captions. They are not preoccupied with appearing right. Authenticity is almost best understood in negative terms. It is achieved when we are *not* doing, when we *stop* trying so hard to be who we think we should be, who others expect us to be. When we allow ourselves to be more as we are. Then we can begin to discover ourselves. The real effort of authenticity is in the work between encounters when we address our unwanted conditioning. When we pry our mask away.

It's happened many times, but I distinctly remember walking out of work one day when a man standing on the street said to me, "You're too pretty not to be smiling. Put a smile on that face, girl." Who could count the number of times that my face, deep in thought or focus, had provoked an unsolicited demand to smile? When I was a cheerleader for a brief stint in middle school, the acrobatics came easy, but my serious face had our coach in the bleachers frantically miming smiles down to me. I was too busy tracking the moves to pretend I was having a blast on top of it all.

"I don't have anything to smile about right now, sir. I'm thinking," I said. "Well, at least smile so I have something to look at," the man on the street said flirtatiously. And even though it irked me, I found myself upturning a corner of my mouth, a toll to exit the conversation.

Inauthenticity is sometimes rewarded. It's a set of defenses learned over time. They can develop out of striving to achieve the visions that were imposed on us. Or we can become someone we're not to protect ourselves from being vulnerable and impacted by other people, a self that is assembled through trauma. People-pleasing is the habitual need to shape-shift according to another's demands, and its root is often gendered or otherwise developed in us by needs we had as children. Many of us learned over time that it was safer to make our own needs secondary to keep someone else happy. When we focus so much on someone else's contentment, we can deprioritize and quiet our own feeling. We lose a sense of who we really are other than who we need to become for another's sake. When we give ourselves away so often, we can start to believe that who we really are is the guilt and shame we feel on the other side of those interactions, which only reinforces our self-abandonment. As a child I learned not to fan the flames of my father's fury, and as an adult I learned to keep anyone else I perceived as volatile happy, and to hide my own life away. When we perceive this disconnect between our true self and the self we're presenting to the world, we can start to understand more about who we are and, from there, build more meaningful and more profound relationships.

I've had clients pendulum swing from one extreme to another in their search for authenticity. An oppressively imposed tendency to please may become for a time a blanket "fuck you" to the requests of others. There's often a kind of freedom in this new conduct, though I've never found that rigidity in behavior or extremes house the authenticity people are looking for. A reaction can beget a reaction that can mask itself as realness, but true authenticity is rarely found in just one way of encountering the world.

There's a practice in somatics classes called "mutual connection," in which two people face each other, bodies mirroring. They take turns placing one hand on the other's chest while practicing both feeling themselves and feeling for the person across from them. As we facilitate the practice, we ask each person if, in making contact with their partner, they have lost awareness of their own sensations. Has their attention tried to merge with the other person, studying their face, their every gesture for clues about the person's desires, or have they, perhaps, retreated into themselves, waiting for the intensity of the moment to subside? Mutuality allows us to feel or at least maintain a curiosity for our own being, our own sense of self, at the same time that we perceive and take in the other person. It's an incredible thing to witness this practice, to see realness unfurl.

On the first day of a somatics course, some people laugh or fidget when they touch the other person. We see some reassuring their partners anxiously and others for whom making eye contact looks physically painful. There's a way to tell that people have hardened something in their own looking, a tightening around the eyes, so that they can see but can't be seen. Just one of the myriad subtle movements our bodies undertake almost imperceptibly to protect us. By the end of the course, after revisiting this practice each day, a hand on their partner's chest, the participants have undergone a transformation. We see changed nervous systems. People able to feel more of themselves, self-adjusting to open up their chests, breathing more deeply. They make room for themselves, their partner, and what's between them. Their bodies have changed to allow themselves to be there both for themselves and for another person.

Mutuality, relationship, is an exchange, an interface with unknown outcomes. It is a reminder of and encounter with the infinite. We usually consign this kind of union to the romantic, believing that the specialness we sense in another person is unique to the one we love. We don't always know that rich relationship and deep connection are available without attraction or desire. That each person possesses as much potential magic as the ones we already love.

When we allow ourselves to be authentic, it's from there that we can be known. Authenticity is the root of vulnerability, of intimacy, of relationship. When we can take off our mask, we invite others to do the same.

BOUNDARIES

"BOUNDARIES ARE THE DISTANCE AT WHICH I can love you and me simultaneously." I wrote these words on Instagram beneath a picture of me with my father after ten years of estrangement. When the quote went viral, I was surprised, but as people started to tell me how it had helped them rethink and remap relationships in their own lives, I came to understand why it resonated.

I had called my father spontaneously after all that time and he had invited me out for breakfast. After I'd stopped speaking to him, I'd assumed that our years of silence would turn into forever, but somewhere in there something shifted for me. The fury I had felt subsided and something unexpected revealed itself: grief and expectation. Over the years, despite the evidence of repeated past disappointments, my hurt feelings had held on to the idea that my father might, or at least should, change, and my rage had spawned more from the heartbreak of him not meeting my needs than from any lingering damage from his behavior. I had wanted him to acknowledge his mistakes. To apologize and make things right. So for years I had fought with him, and even when I stopped speaking to him, I had fought him in my mind until I found the strength to accept that he might never change. And it was then that the foundation cracked and the walls came tumbling down. I grieved. For the child who had never felt safe, who had internalized that they were unlovable because they'd never felt love in the way they dreamed it was possible. Finally, I felt the emotions I had been protecting myself from, that I had stopped myself from feeling, and it made room for me to get down to the work of tending to myself. I started to crave a different kind of love, love that didn't require me to question my lovability or to try to make myself lovable for someone else. Love that strived to meet my needs. Most important, I started a primary relationship with myself and learned how to attend to me. I took myself out and did things that I liked. I took responsibility for myself, my anger, and my joy. I learned how to maintain my integrity, not compromise it.

That was the person who picked up the phone after ten years and called their dad out of a curiosity that just showed up when I let him go. In my pep talk to myself in the car outside the diner, I kept saying, I choose what to share, I choose what I respond to, I choose when to leave. I see people all the time who bring others back into their lives after distance and assume that the relationship and their proximity to each other should revert to what it once was. Instead, ruptures should inform the shape of relationships going forward. We should relate differently based on what's happened, now that we've learned something about who the other actually is and who we are. If not, we risk falling into the same patterns that didn't work before.

I met my father at a local breakfast spot where seniors and veterans gather back in my hometown. It was packed with people and filled with the sounds of heavy diner coffee mugs landing on tables. When I walked in, he put one arm around me and squeezed and I offered my forehead for a kiss. We got a two-seater table right in the middle. I looked at his hands, a larger version of my own. His smile began with the creases around his eyes the same way mine did. He'd aged; his breathing was more labored now. I was nervous, but grounded. He was familiar to my bones, though I wasn't sure I'd missed him. I watched him as he shook hands with his buddies and they patted him on the back. We laughed together at the comments he made behind their backs when they walked away. "How have you been?" I asked. "Good!" he said, and launched into a rundown of his recent accomplishments and updates on who had gotten into what trouble lately. He never mentioned how long it had been, how different I must look after all that time. He spoke as if no time had passed at all, though this was the first meal we'd had as two adults. From across the table I took him in, noting the words and nodding, but mostly I was feeling the chasm of what was unspoken.

At the end of the meal, my father got too comfortable and started in on my mother and their relationship. I felt myself begin to brace; my breathing shallowed and my chest that had started to soften hardened again. I was trying to keep his words out of me. My body was communicating my limit. I decided to leave. I had found the point where I would need to compromise my own care in order to stay.

These are boundaries. When we decide the shape and nature of our relationships. When we are not forced into closeness because of expectations or history, but we choose according to our comfort. We get to move forward with the knowledge of our history, following a path of our own making. I framed boundaries as love when I first wrote the phrase because that was the measure for me: At what distance could I maintain care for both my father and me? Because despite the pain, I found that I loved him.

Boundaries are not about control; they are a way of resetting power dynamics in relationships, of restoring our sense of agency and choice. Maybe most important, boundaries are how we shelter our authenticity, our real selves, and they are essential as we build relationship with one another. We can look to our bodies for indication. If you've ever been trapped in conversation with someone who talks in a flood, not picking up on your cues, your shuffling feet, downcast eyes, but just keeps on talking, then if you're like me, you might start to shrink yourself, your listening, your shoulders drawn in, and begin to back away. Your boundary has been compromised. Not only is your body communicating transgression to the overstepper, it is communicating it to you. Do you know how to listen to the boundaries of your body? Do you know how to leave when the time is right for you? Your body holds the answer. You just have to listen to it.

Boundaries are how we stay and feel intact. Balanced relationships do not require our escape. Nor can relationships thrive when we only impose, flood, fill the room with our thoughts and stories without leaving space for the unexpected to arrive. Balance is not a stagnant state; it, too, is a dance, an ever-fluctuating way of being. There's an ebb and flow, a meeting in the middle. Relationship at its most mutual, most just, is negotiated.

Years ago, I was on an airplane and the man sitting next to me opened his newspaper so wide that it covered my view, his arm just missing the bridge of my nose. My phone was no longer visible, and I found myself looking directly at an opinion piece in his *New York Times*. I sat and stewed, getting angrier by the second, debating whether or not to make a bold show about manspreading, but instead I sat there quietly, waiting for him to notice my anger. He never did. After he was done reading, the man closed the paper and spoke kindly to me. I was stunned. His spread wasn't actively malicious as much as it was indicative of his expectations of the world. I imagined he had been taught that his space could intersect mine without permission, that I would bend to the contours of his body. Sometimes we think our bounds extend beyond our own bodies; that is, sometimes we feel balanced when we are in control of others' spaces, too. This can be a survival response or it may be historical residue. Of course, I can only assume the man's training, but it activated in me a familiar story, one in which a white man on his way to a meeting might have gotten used to other people moving around him and his needs. These gendered and racialized expectations about space and relationship are part of our history, our politics. Who can take it up and who adjusts or is pushed to the side. Who expects to be listened to and is, and who is ignored, silenced, or discounted. And when we can honor and express boundaries, ours and other people's, especially in our interpersonal or work relationships with one another, we can escape our learned behaviors about whose boundaries can be bulldozed or why we need to deny our own. Boundaries require us to rework and restructure relationships for the sake of connection, for deep mutuality. How might that man on the plane and I have met had we been taught that our bodies were both autonomous and related? Would I have felt comfortable speaking up and reminding him of who we were to each other? Would he have been able to let himself sense my life there just as much as his own? Boundaries open up the possibility of mutuality in real time. They don't undo our history, but they are the choice to meet one another honestly through it, even for a moment.

What if we could feel our way through relationship? If our physical integrity, our ability to relate without our defenses up, could become the basis for how we build and maintain relationship? It will take some of us, in some places, to voice our limits and our needs rather than to simmer in resentment. It will require some of us, at some times, to make ourselves more sensitive, more aware and open to listening, more capable of real connection and intimacy with the other. And it may hurt. Receiving boundaries in a relationship where we've expected space may feel like rejection or denial—and that feeling is our teacher about our own entitlement. Expressing boundaries and feeling the urge to cross them to appease someone else is our teacher of our codependency. All of this may be inherited, or it may be learned, but all of it can be remade. The choice is ours.

I have gotten pushback on the language of boundaries from people involved in community organizing and from people in healing communities. I've heard from both that boundaries reinforce individualism and misguided beliefs about separateness. But for me this is too simplistic. Our bodies are encased in skin that is both barrier and porous. It lets things in and it keeps things out. We are both individual and collective. And as much as boundaries differentiate, they are evidence of our impact on one another, of our interrelatedness, not a denial of it. They are how we shape the relational space between us with each of our needs. They are not barriers to keep us apart, more an invitation into knowing who each of us is. They arise from us understanding who we are, where we come from, our limits and our needs, and enable us to welcome relationship with others from a place of balance, of safety. From our true selves.

My original quote on boundaries toured the world and brought back to me so many stories of how people have used it. I was told once that it was spoken at a funeral to describe a woman who lived life on her own terms. People have shared how it helped them separate or divorce with dignity and care. Others have told me how it revived and recentered their friendships and partnerships on love. And one man shared at an event that it changed his relationships with his children.

He was teaching them that they could have boundaries even in their family and was expressing more of his own. When care for ourselves and one another is at the core of our relationships, what's possible changes.

TRUST

RECENTLY, I'VE BEEN CALLED IN to several organizations to help address issues of mistrust among staff. I've been seeing this a lot lately. Organizations fracturing, working relationships breaking down, missions derailed because of missteps that have gone unaddressed and led to entrenched barriers, depleting the trust that people really need between one another in order to work together. To me this phenomenon of corroding trust between individuals makes sense when we look at the backdrop of our times, at the sense of betrayal many people feel toward systems they were once so attached to, that they depend on for care and protection, systems that have let them down. Trust in big, all-powerful, supposedly benevolent forces of the state, in corporations, and in the economic system of capitalism is waning. There is abundant evidence that the needs of working people factor less and less into the decision-making of our elected officials. The scales have tipped so far toward greed that their primary job now seems to be to say just enough to placate or distract. And, in a country set up for white dominance, when those who benefit most from its prevailing structure see institutions failing even them, their concern incentivizes them to blame and mistrust the others they are told are taking their God-given status.

I think, perhaps because I am a Black, queer, nonbinary woman and have researched history enough to see that the foundation for this trust in institutions was always tenuous at best, I have felt less destabilized in these periods of upheaval. I have always been more cautious about where I place my trust. Yet, as societal mistrust increases, I have seen a correlating rise in *interpersonal* mistrust. In people abandoning trust itself even as a necessary value, adopting instead a pervasive suspicion in every aspect of their lives, an "if in doubt, shoot" kind of mindset. Misinformation and fearmongering campaigns instigated through social media and news networks are designed to elicit exactly this sentiment, the feeling that we don't know whom to trust, while clearly dictating a set of convenient enemies, an outlet for our dissatisfaction and disorientation. It is usually those seeking equitable treatment or rights, those upsetting the beloved status quo, who are represented as untrustworthy characters: Black, queer, trans, migrant. But trust itself is not the issue here, and refusing to grant trust anywhere breeds in us confusion, fear, and isolation. This interplay between public and private trust makes it harder to solve societal problems and create change.

Trust is the bedrock of human coordination, collaboration, and repair, and without it, as social beings, it can be hard for us to accomplish much of anything with one another. When trust is not present, we get stuck, unable to act, unable to build, unable to work toward human achievements. Trust is the connective tissue, the lubricant, that makes things go. But how do we generate and maintain trust, especially in times when mistrust threatens to isolate us from one another and keep us locked in ineffectiveness?

My kid, Amaya, is a reckless cannonball in my home. As she started to crawl, I watched her begin to venture off toward things that caught her interest, a broken wheel that had found its way under the couch, or my headphones placed riskily within her reach. She'd reliably look to the object she was about to grab and then glance over at me, as though asking permission, but also, mostly, informing me of what she was about to do. The look told me that I was her anchor. She trusted me to protect her, to caution her, to be there as she explored. But it also seemed as if she were asking me to trust her to take the risk. She teaches me that trust is developmental, ingrained, and reciprocal. We reach for one another from the beginning.

Charles Feltman, author of *The Thin Book of Trust*, defines trust this way, as choosing to make something you value vulnerable to another person's actions. Trust is a risk we take with one another to do something bigger than we could have done alone. Our personal histories play an important role here, as whatever we've come to embody or believe about safety often dictates how we trust. I've been on an airplane a number of times when, even before the plane has taken off, the person next to me has confessed to me something deeply personal. A woman once told me I had a face that made her feel like she could tell me anything—though my face that day was mostly sleepy. Some of it, I'm sure, has to do with my years of training as a therapist, perhaps a sense of receptiveness, but some of it is connected, too, with an unfounded extension of trust. If we've learned through trauma that crossing our own boundaries is the only way to belong, or to create safety and relationship, then we might develop a tendency to overshare or overtrust. By the same token, if we have gotten hurt and taken the lesson that relationship and revealing our inner self are dangerous, or if the people we needed to rely on did not show up for us, we might find it hard to extend trust anywhere in our lives, even when it might be deserved. At work we might struggle to trust our team, or at home we might not trust the people we love, even when they are devoted to us. We may think that it is self-sufficiency that keeps us from collaborating or from sharing the weight of what we carry with someone who might be willing. How we trust is shaped by our experiences.

Trust is a two-way street. Just as we need to be able to trust others to build connection, we need to be trustworthy for others to trust us. That means being reliable, doing what we say we will to the best of our ability, and honoring relationships where trust is being built with care and communication. Most of us assess ourselves as more trustworthy than everyone else we know—and probably as more trustworthy than we are. We have front row seats to our intentions, and we can see all those good (to us) reasons for our mistakes or missteps. Without this same information, it's much easier to see other people as chronically unreliable or their slipups as malicious. We are convinced they disappoint us because of some deep character flaw. Most of us expect to be trusted and only measure or judge trustability in other people or institutions, rarely in ourselves. It may take a midlife crisis or spiritual awakening for most of us to take stock of our own trustworthiness. But it's important to consider. Do the people around us find us trustworthy? Do we inspire trust in others? Does our word coincide with our action? How can we be more intentional about being trustworthy?

Just as who and how we trust is often shaped by our interpersonal experiences, it is also conditioned in us through the way that society assigns value to people. Any society that ranks people based on race or gender or any other arbitrary characteristic teaches that trust should be allocated not by personal merit but by how closely one conforms to social norms—and so trust becomes little more than the reification of existing social structures and mythologies. In this way, we are either entitled to trust or denied it categorically, regardless of what we do or how we show up. In my work, I've often seen this at play: Trust is given easily to some people simply because they look the part, while others are mistrusted or overlooked because they don't. I've been the recipient of ungrounded trust in some scenarios; in others I've been second-guessed or disregarded. I've also seen the ways in which people who are repeatedly mistrusted, doubted, or betrayed can start to withhold their trust in others. It's a cycle. And it causes damage in our personal relationships and within our communities and systems. We all carry with us our habits and personal stories about trust because it is easier than being vulnerable enough to build and maintain trust. But if we truly want to transform ourselves and work with others, we must be willing to face—and change—our habits.

OUR RELATIONSHIPS CAN BE FREED SOME from the expectations imposed by history and oppression when they are given more room, prioritized, and centered. When as Black people, or as women, or men, or Brown people, or whoever we might be, we allow ourselves to feel honestly, authentically, and to be open to meeting one another in relationship. Relationship is not some transcendent space. It is the trenches. It is risky and implicating to fully connect with someone. We don't bypass history and what we've inherited from it, but instead we hold it and all the ways it's taught us to find safety in distance, or to believe in superiority and inferiority myths. We hold those stories up next to what we really feel, where our bodies pull toward and where they recoil. We investigate if our impulses are the result of our conditioning or are a deeper truth. We make mistakes and recover. But running from our history, ignoring it, flattening it, denying what we feel when we are close, does nothing to have us really meet one another. It's like trying to hold the ocean at a distance. It just makes us dishonest and more isolated from ourselves, from one another. But by making use of the knowledge of our history, using our power and position to make it safer for real things to be shared between us, we surrender to what is ultimately uncontrollable and filled with endless possibility, the terrain of relationship.

Living with history is as much a spiritual practice as an embodied one, a practice really of inviting the past to tell us how it has shaped us, what gifts it has offered us, and what limitations it has imposed on us. What does our training allow us to do, and what does it prohibit? Who does it tell us we need to be most of the time, and for whom? Who does it tell us others need to be for the world to make sense? Are we willing to know it to that degree, and are we willing to lay the scripts down for something else? For authentic encounters, in all their unpredictability. For the bumps and challenges of real-time relationship in which we get to find out who we are and enter into the realm of living beings who find growth, transformation, and connection to be their primary tasks. When we are able to live with our history, there's a possibility in relationship to dissolve the isolation that defensiveness has moved us toward and to experience the wonder of intimacy, understanding, and being truly seen. There's the possibility that we might find that when our relationships are nimble and honest, and we are emotionally sturdy enough to be in them, we can build much bigger things than we could have alone, that we can withstand more pressure together. Such relationships can transform us—and they are the key to transforming society.

The kid I was at the mall that day, crouching through the aisles, didn't have the language to describe what I suddenly understood when my presence parted traffic. I saw then that most of the time we act out scripts that have been offered to us. We play our roles in the show. I got a glimpse that day that there was something more to who I was, and who I and others could be with one another. Our relationships can be full of everything life is. Our relationships can be powerful places of transformation. It only takes moving out from underneath what is expected and into what is real.

5

ENGAGE WITH THE WORLD

Anything could happen, and whether we act or not has everything to do with it.
—Rebecca Solnit, *Hope in the Dark*

THE FIRST SPRING AFTER WE MOVED TO RURAL NORTH CAROLINA, what had been a modest gardening practice developed into something wilder and more consuming. My hands were daily in the dirt, planting seeds, weeding, plucking pests from squash, harvesting, and tasting what tumbled to the ground. Our hard work was rewarded in abundance, in figs, collards, and tomatoes. But the unexpected returns were what was shown to me of myself. My tendency to over-effort on simple tasks showed up when I tugged too hard on almost-ready okra and broke the stem. Slower, more intentional effort preserved my energy and kept the plant intact. And when, after I had staved off deer for most of the summer, they broke through my rigged fishing-line fence and cleaned us out in one night, the disappointment and anger I felt were clear lessons on properly constructed boundaries and impermanence. Composting taught me the most, though—how the discards, the rotting parts, could become fertile ground for the next year's harvest. I'd visit the compost bin when someone came to me with a seemingly intractable conflict, or when I otherwise felt at my end. How, I would ask, can this mess become soil?

The garden was more challenging than any social media account had let on with their polished pictures of people in stain-free jeans. I would never have known if not for the time I spent there on my own knees. I was sweaty most days, sometimes bloody, but suddenly savoring every leaf, bulb, and fruit as a miracle. There's something about digging in, giving yourself over to an activity, that infuses everything that comes from it with more significance. Every meal we ate had more meaning. We savored our food. Pointed out each thing we'd grown on our plates and swore we could taste our efforts. It taught me a lot; namely, that you begin with an idea, a vision, but it's the everyday work that produces the real lessons and the real change. The space between inspiration and what we might call the result is where things become surprisingly unwieldy, and beautiful, painful, and miraculous. Mainly, it's where we become someone different from who we were when we began. We enter the same process when we decide to take some kind of political action, to make some kind of change within our society. There's the point at which we can see the issue and imagine something better, then there's another point at which we do something about it, even if in small ways. That's really how we transform platitudes into experience, outrage into action, and these processes necessarily change us, returning our effort to us as power.

Our lives get richer when we start to metabolize and heal the pain and the stories that live in us. We become more present, our lives more felt. We have more access to the experience of relationship. Instead of existing in perpetual reactivity, we spend more of our time in the vast now, where connection and possibility reside, which is all worthwhile on its own—life for life's sake, as my teacher Alta Starr says. And yet we can't maintain our healing if the conditions around us don't shift in some meaningful way, if the pressures keep mounting and we keep losing what sustains us. When a president or politician says it's time to heal after another egregious action by a police officer, they usually mean it's time for the community to quiet down, to take our rage indoors, to stuff it into whatever corner of our bodies or lives we can. Never do they mean it's time for a real reckoning, for repair, for a restructuring of the systems that caused the incident in the first place, which is what real healing, tending to the injury, would truly mean. In order for healing to happen at scale, on a societal level, we need tangible and significant changes to our institutions and to the underlying culture we live in. To get there, we all have to dirty our hands and become involved in the making of the world in far deeper ways than we've been taught are possible. And it all has to be done with one another.

We are sold an approach to healing that prioritizes reprieve and disengagement, retreat and solitude, peace and calm. Of course, unplugging gives us the space we sometimes desperately need to reassess and listen, to hear ourselves, our own heartbeats in the silence. But if we believe that our wholeness requires long-term disconnection from the world, we run the risk of mistaking what is comfortable for what is healing, a sense of control with safety, and reinforcing separation and isolation. It is only a temporary escape, seeking higher ground as the shore recedes.

And what about the return? Disconnection does not address what makes our lives unlivable in the first place. Healing in solitude eventually brings us home only to realize that what causes us pain, what causes many others pain, are issues much bigger than our singular lives—and those issues remain: income disparity, generational trauma, isolation, the slights and violence of being made a marginalized other. Such widespread systemic and historical injustice limits our capacity, and even when we are able to address trauma through individual healing, it's not enough. Only when we come together to shape, dismantle, and rebuild the world can we start to end the ongoing cycles of collective trauma caused by systems obsessed with profit and not the well-being of all humans and the planet. We can't change the world if we do not heal what has become embodied in us, and we cannot truly heal if the conditions that break and isolate us don't change, too.

The majority of people I've worked with in a therapeutic setting have been survivors of childhood sexual violence, a number indicative of a crisis we have never really tried to understand. Nearly every time that someone discloses their truth to me in a session, the words are said in shame. Long after the incident, they hold on to the story that they should have known better or should have told someone, that they are somehow to blame for what was done to them. Over the years, I've supported a lot of people, helping them to release some of the self-blame and shame, to feel some semblance of safety, and to enhance their experience of love and trust in others. But I also know that to really care about the harm that happened to them, I have to pay attention to how frequently

these stories are told and how similar they are. To how com-
monplace and widespread this silent abuse of children is, to
what it says about our culture and the people it creates. We
each feel our pain acutely in our bodies, but our experiences
are rarely as isolated as they seem. And when we put the onus
on the individual to transform but ask nothing of the culture
that makes this abuse endemic, we do nothing to stop it from
happening again.

In 2018, I worked with the Chicago Torture Justice Center (CTJC), an organization that addresses the trauma of police violence by providing survivors with access to individual
healing services while building community and working to
dismantle systems that harm. It was born out of a reparations
ordinance passed by the city in 2015 in response to years of
community campaigning and testimony at the United Na-
tions. Statements there described the torture of nearly two
hundred people, primarily Black men, at the hands of Officer
Jon Burge and his team of detectives at the Chicago Police
Department. Between 1972 and 1991, this police violence
led to multiple forced confessions, and many men were in-
carcerated for years, decades even, for crimes they did not
commit. The reparations ordinance allocated city resources
to address the ongoing trauma of survivors and their families,
and CTJC was formed soon after, becoming the only organization in the United States dedicated to addressing incidents
of domestic torture.

My colleagues Mark-Anthony Johnson and Francisca
Porchas Coronado and I, along with CTJC staff and members, created a politicized healing framework to shape clinical
treatment—in the form of individual and group mental health
sessions—and community-building work. Our aim was not

only to help heal the trauma felt by people impacted by police violence and incarceration but also to tackle the systems that had caused and were still causing oppression. The work that CTJC does is like nothing I've seen before from either therapeutic or movement spaces. It is holistic and comprehensive, treating the trauma of their community and advocating for justice and safety. One mother joined the organization soon after her son was shot dead by police at just twenty years old. She started coming to their Freedom Songbook group, a weekly gathering where survivors and their families sing Black freedom songs together and write their own. She came, she said, distraught, feeling deeply alone and helpless after losing her child. After a year of singing with this group, her blood pressure had dropped, her hair was growing back, her appetite had returned, and she could, for the first time since her son was killed, sleep through the night. CTJC has been building this model for the last few years, providing care and ritual for healing, for growth. They've created a strong community of dedicated survivors who are now beginning to develop a campaign to hold accountable the rest of the officers who committed torture. Their personal healing created the capacity for the organizing and the desire to create a campaign that will bring justice for the larger community. The two go hand in hand.

Healing is necessary for us to care for our lives and how we feel in them, and it's especially potent when coupled with our action and engagement in something bigger than us. So it is not one or the other, healing ourselves or ending oppression. We have to engage in both.

. . .

MY GRANDMOTHER WAS A POLL WORKER, and when my parents and I arrived at the elementary school cafeteria turned voting station on Election Day, I'd spot her there, presiding over a folding table of ballots. Voting was a major neighborhood event. Everyone was there greeting everyone else with an air of formality we only ever saw after church service. My grandmother would be in her Sunday best, looking more official and dutiful than I'd ever seen her. She'd lean over the table, look me in the eye, and impart how important it was for us to vote, how we'd fought for this right. She'd hand me a kids' ballot that made me feel official, too, and I'd take it to sit in the children's corner while we watched with some reverence the procession of adults.

Doing the math, I know now that my grandmother was nearly forty years old before the Voting Rights Act was passed and so she must have carried viscerally the import of the act and the reality of life without it. For a long time, I misunderstood what I believe now was at the core of her message to me. I took it then to mean that election days were our sole opportunities to engage politically with the system and so voting was important because it was our only democratic outlet. Only later did I really understand that voting rights did not come to pass with President Johnson's sweep of a pen, but from decades of pressure from people just like my grandmother—regular, everyday, committed, brilliant people bringing petitions to church, calling on their neighbors, orchestrating civil disobedience, and organizing their communities. That side of politics was hidden to me. For my grandmother's generation of Black people, voting was a necessary component of citizenship, of having some semblance of power, but it was also a symbol and reminder. It was a reminder of what we could do when we were organized, when we came together. Election Day was as much about the ballot as it was the community, the ritual of our gathering to shape the conditions impacting our lives. These moments of human connection around a cause have always been a pivotal point: the politics with a small p that happen every day.

The personal is political and the political lives in our personal interactions no matter how much we might wish we could cleave them apart. At times I've felt suffocated by this. Politics can make everything we do seem so weighty with responsibility; it can be hard to move or think things through without the guilt of needing to get it right. Our lives can seem too enmeshed, the world too lopsided for any action we take to even seem worthwhile. But if we can drop the idea that politics means getting everything perfect or fixing everything we see, there's a freedom in it, too. The freedom that comes from the privilege of shaping the world around us. To me, politics is simply how we make decisions about the resources we have. Who we decide is excluded and on what basis. It's our actions and what we take responsibility for. It's what we choose to do about the messes history has left us. In a time when especially national politics, big-P politics, can feel so disempowering, overwhelming, looking more deeply at what's around each of us—what political decisions and actions we *can* make, what pressure our community can apply, what new way we can dream up—gives us the opportunity to feel the agency available to us in the risk of taking action and building power. It's an opportunity to demand more from the world and create more in it.

Lately, people lament that the political has seeped into our daily lives, into our homes. We are either living through a campaign season or preparing for the crisis and escalation of the next. Once-peaceful family meals have become battle-fields, with people reciting cable news talking points or conspiracy theories from Facebook or their favorite YouTuber. National politics has breached civil bounds, and we are outraged, fearful, reactive, and divided; yet, for all our preoccupation with the spectacle of politics, rights regress and income gaps continue to widen, and political power remains located somewhere far away. For many of us, politics is a game played out in Washington by politicians who seem far removed from the realities of our lives, who have lost touch with our needs. They are unreachable and unaccountable, and we are left with our anxiety and no apparent way of stopping what is coming toward us. The reactive state sparked by our fear can cause some of us to spiral in panic or doom or chronically leave the moment in dissociation or coping. And we start to believe that it is this reactivity that is necessary for our survival. Our bodies give up on the possibility that there is another way.

The force that brings about political change is power. Martin Luther King, Jr., once defined power as the relative ability to achieve purpose. The more power we have in any given situation, the easier it is to do what we intend. The less power, the harder it becomes to exercise choice over our lives and what happens in them. Power is necessary for anything to happen, though many of us are raised to fear it. Because of how we've seen people use the power we give them, we assume that power is only domination and exclusion, not generosity and protection. The test of power, how we show what guides it, is in how we wield it. To me, the root of any power is in the body, specifically in our ability to be embodied in a way that organizes our cells and our self to act out a vision. As trauma disconnects parts of our knowing and our bodies, it can make our actions less congruent, and it can diminish our realization of our own power. But power is not only an individual's expression. It is first felt in the alignment of our own bodies, then multiplied and amplified in our syncopation, in our coordination with one another. We cultivate power in ourselves, and we build power when we work together.

IN MANY WAYS, I WAS lucky to be brought into social justice organizing young, just after college. I'm not sure exactly who gave me the idea that I could change anything about how the world worked, but I knew something had to give. The first campaign I worked on was for affordable housing in Oakland, led by a coalition of local community groups. New developments in the city were pricing out the people who had long lived there, threatening to uproot communities and disrupt lives. I had grown up with some housing instability, and at the time I was living in a communal house with ten other people; the room my girlfriend and I shared was a living area converted into a bedroom by tapestries hung over the entryways. That campaign was the first space where I could share stories of what had happened in my own life, of what I had seen around me, and have them be heard, where I listened to similar stories spoken without shame. It restored my sense of agency; that I could, that *we* could, effect change relevant to our own lives.

We spent months door-knocking, talking to our neighbors about housing insecurity and rising rent costs, about what it means to have nowhere to live. Our groups spent the weekends asking local residents what affordable meant to them, and with that knowledge we proposed that a certain percentage of new developments remain accessible to the people who already lived in the city, not just to the tech transplants they were trying to draw in. I went to city council meetings and offered testimony along with other community members. We met with officials and found out quickly who was aligned with us and who wasn't, who was motivated by concern for their constituents and who was in the pockets of the housing developers. I learned in that process about how local politics work. I saw that the decisions made were not handed down from on high but were always negotiated. The people who sat on those councils were elected and could be replaced by people just like us. And our involvement, though it didn't result in exactly the win we'd hoped for, changed the outcome. Community pressure secured more housing units for those with reduced incomes than had originally been proposed, allowing more local residents the opportunity to stay, people who might otherwise have been pushed out of their homes. We'd done it by working together, building our power, and taking action. It was more than any of us could have done alone. This is small-p politics in action.

To get involved like this, it's helpful to know where to start. To begin with, we might first understand that we are all embedded in networks, that we exist in systems, as interacting and interrelated elements of a unified whole—we are not the free-floating individuals our society might have us believe. We depend on one another. We are one part of something bigger in so many different places, our families, friend groups, communities, places of work, or faith communities. Though we may not realize it, these are all systems. Our family is its own distinct organism with a shape and way of being, and we

are surrounded by other systems like schools and prisons that
we may not think directly impact us but that also influence
our lives in many ways. These various interconnected systems
ripple outward from us, an ever-expanding network of people.
At the center are the smaller systems, our families and ex-
tended families, and then they spread, the number of people
within them growing, perhaps to a neighborhood, made up of
our family and lots of other families, and then to a region en-
compassing scores of families along with our own throughout
a broader community. As we start to take action across these
larger systems, it becomes impossible to do so alone. We
need other people to make institutional and cultural change.
We can't transform an entire school or healthcare system alone.
We need a network of more and more people, like-minded
people who share our visions and are willing to risk involvement and work together. When we appreciate that, it is easier
to see how we can start to make change, by reaching out to
others, and through small steps at a time.

While these systems are sometimes the sites of both individual and collective trauma, each of these sites, these systems, is also a potential place of action and transformation.
Just as they shape us, they are places that can be shaped and
reshaped, rebuilt and reworked, abolished and replaced. No
system is static or infinite. Knowing this is powerful. Even in
our families, someone marries, another dies, a secret is spoken
for the first time, and the dynamics suddenly shift. A school
in our town bans certain history books. A city council makes
plans for a highway that will run through the core of a town,
decimating local businesses and wildlife. A movement springs
up after years of disquiet and it changes legislation and language. It brings people together. The bigger the barrier, the

more of us it requires to change—but the possibility is there when we see our place and power in the systems we inhabit.

The clinic where I worked when Trayvon Martin was killed did not have a break room, so the therapists crowded around the front desk in between appointments. Once the other therapists and clients were in their rooms with white noise machines humming in the hallways, we'd gather. We'd talk about race and economic systems, oppression and gender. About our role as therapists and what it meant to be providing support to people whose issues could only be fully resolved systemically. I believed very much in the power of the skills we were developing in our clients, and I also knew that we therapists had to think about our power and role differently from the way we'd been taught. Pushing the idea that everything could be faced alone, even with the help of therapy, could leave people overwhelmed and isolated. These conversations had become even more urgent in the wake of Trayvon's murder. Why not, I'd say, encourage people to protest as part of their treatment? Why shouldn't we have a reading group for therapists, so that we could really understand what was happening in our world? Why shouldn't we know where our power lay and use it?

To initiate change, we can only begin where we are and as whoever we are right now. As a therapist, as part of a larger institution, this was where I could start. We are all a part of something bigger than ourselves, a neighborhood, a geographic community, maybe a school. We are a part of a race, a gender, a faith, a profession. Each of these sites or communities bears its own challenges and responsibilities to the whole. Each has its own systems and norms, and each is a place where we hold power. When we turn to those places, bring people together, or join what exists, we move out of our little worlds into a bigger one. When we share experience, we create community, a foundation for change.

I might differ on this point with friends and colleagues who are more rigorous organizers and activists than I, but I believe there's something worthwhile in the effort to transform any and all systems that we are involved in. Our family systems are a valuable place of practice, as are our places of work, and the state institutions and their systems—education, healthcare, housing—require our action, too. I cannot see the world simply as what is big or what is small. Our world is entangled with multiple forces acting on us, and we act, very often, in accordance with our conditioning by these forces. So let's begin where we are. Take the awareness we have and let it be grown, expanded, and nurtured by the awareness and commitment of others.

When we engage, we collaborate with the world in its creation. We are able to establish and clarify our shared values, our visions, and give meaning to what surrounds us—which in turn shapes us and those around us. In contrast, to disengage from the world of power and resources is to allow others to mold culture and determine meaning for our lives. To dictate how we should look, what we should own, and the world we live in becomes increasingly divorced from what we really care about and more connected to the fluctuations of markets and our insecurities. Growing food has taught me about plants, what grows well, which creatures are my competition. I am part of an ecosystem. When I visit the farmers market now, I know what it takes to grow something from seed to fruit, all the decisions and care that go into it. My world has grown wider, more full. I notice now where food doesn't grow, where concrete has replaced fertile ground, where produce aisles are sparse and farmers markets don't visit. I can wonder how food deserts came to be, why there are neighborhoods and blocks that a city or county might choose to divest from. What the people there eat and how it shapes their well-being. When I am invested in the world, it shows itself to me with a new clarity—and I can be more ready to respond.

Political theorist Hannah Arendt called on philosophers to be involved in the world, to renounce lives of seclusion. She believed that in the space we generate together, where we struggle politically, where we engage democratically with one another, we bring our voice and experience to decisions that are made, we shape what is done and for what reason, and in that way, we go about the process of world making. We decide together what is sacred and we hold it as such.

When Confederate monuments came down during the Freedom Summer of 2020, though only seventy out of the country's seven hundred were removed, it was a powerful rebuke of white supremacist beliefs and worldviews. Monuments are important. They're physical reminders, insisting on a history and asserting a set of values. They declare the victors even if they are the ones who technically lost the war, and they never belong only to the past; monuments have a vision embedded in them, too. Most Confederate monuments were built long after the Civil War had ended with the sole intent of glorifying the Confederacy and holding it up as an ideal. They were not simple memorials to fallen soldiers but grand statues to repellent leaders built in town squares and in front of public buildings so that they would be seen by everyone, not flattened into textbooks or hidden in museums. They beg history to repeat itself.

Why wouldn't racism persist when it's what we choose to enshrine?

I wondered when the monuments came down whether new ones would be erected in their place. Whether we could look history in the face and decide to preserve the lessons in another way. Such as honoring freedom and resistance and courage, with newly created monuments to Maroons or abolitionists springing up in the place of fallen enslavers. Or monuments memorializing rebellions against colonizers, reminding us how to reject domination over our bodies and land. What we remember, and how, does not have to be imposed on us. We can have a say in who we decide to canonize and in how we commemorate those moments—and those actions can guide us into another kind of future, one that we are shaping.

There hasn't been enough time yet for history to examine this, but I'll say it here. While social media has been an incredible tool for activation around social change movements, it has been a real obstacle to engagement, a scenario that has worked well for some agendas and proved a barrier for others. As the most dangerous elements of the right have shown us, it is much easier to make people fearful online than it is to make people willing and able to understand the complexities of systems and take thoughtful and coordinated action to address them. This was a tension many of us felt in Black Lives Matter and was an ongoing internal discussion within the broader movement.

The power of social media was smartly harnessed early

on to connect people all over the world under a shared banner. Across the globe, millions of people found meaning in the phrase and the assessment that Black people's lives were as precious as anyone's. But breadth isn't the same as depth. Within Black Lives Matter and in the Movement for Black Lives more broadly, people grappled with the challenge that while social media can turn people out into the streets it is not always the best tool for prolonged and deep engagement on an issue. It isn't designed to build trust over time, or to inspire nuanced explanation of complex issues, nor does it generously and generatively step into conflict that stretches and teaches us, or require or encourage deep connection.

Instead, it is designed for outrage, for the impulsive, the momentary. It cultivates the reactionary in us and can attract the most reactionary of us. We get the dopamine hit while our repost signifies that, for at least the present moment, we are the good person with the right politics who we aspire to be. But the process is less able to sustain attention and build relationship across difference. We are less able to commit to anything deeply because the intellectual and emotional energy it takes to stay the course of any particular issue is crowded out by whatever adrenalizes us next. People move from centering Black lives to impending climate crises to the threat of global war in seconds. These phenomena are not unrelated—in fact, they are deeply connected through the tendrils of our economic and cultural systems—but our way of engaging them becomes siloed and based on panic and distraction, a function of the media we use. Overwhelmed by constant saturation, we lose the wherewithal to prioritize how we might meaningfully engage with issues from where and who we are.

We often forget that we can start by taking a moment to listen in to ourselves. What is within your purview to do, and who can you join with to extend your reach and build your power?

The body that can engage in building what we truly need, that can sustain action over time, is something different from the distractible, unmoored body manipulated by social media. It is a rhythmic body, undulating, present, feeling, capable of curiosity, awe, rage, and love. It is a body that can generate a safety for ourselves and others, that along with the despair can tap into the possibility that if we commit and are willing to change and allow others the same grace we just might win.

OUR EFFORTS TO RESHAPE STRUCTURES and the world around us aren't only altruistic, if they could ever be called that, but are one of the ways we build the community we need. Many of us feel alone. Even when we are interconnected by systems, we may not perceive our connection. At the height of Covid-19's sweep, when we still had very little information about how the virus spread, I saw many clients who were suddenly isolated, stranded in their lives. There were some who had to work outside the home, but the fear of infection had narrowed their day-to-day. Some I knew hadn't left their houses in weeks. One person confided to me in a vulnerable conversation, "I'm not really sure I'm even human anymore." And it struck me then how much we need one another, not as an abstract, but as a bodily fact. Human beings are a highly social species, and our nervous systems are wired to have other people around us. We do better physically and mentally when we have a strong social support system. Listening to my clients, I knew the most important intervention I could make was to be a consistent point of connection for them, and for other people in my life who needed it, to check in on the basics and hold space for their much more exposed desire now to belong.

Getting involved politically opens us up to the messy world of other people, which may seem frightening, but we've seen that we need other people for our own well-being, and we also need people for safety and for building power. We need people because we grow in relationship. When we dig in together, when our ideas are tested and held up to another's light, we become more than we could have been on our own. As we engage with one another, our ideas develop and deepen. Just like the food I've grown has stories inside of it. Of trial and error, of adaptations I've made. Of adjustments and learning and starting over. Harvesting the food was no certainty; it was the process, the journey, that made it so. And importantly, as we create change together, as we take on the transformation of systems from ones that harm into ones that attend to our living, as we insist on our visions together, as we disagree and align, support one another and learn to risk, we end up along the way creating the community we need.

Getting involved in something larger than ourselves has the potential to offer a kind of healing, too. In the same way that we need other people to make a greater impact, we often need to engage and connect with the world to heal collective trauma. The trauma we experience on a personal level—such as being dehumanized as a Black or queer person—can be felt at a collective level, too, and individual healing alone may not be enough to address the bigger systemic issues. On the night that George Zimmerman was acquitted, or when Breonna Taylor or George Floyd or Tyre Nichols was killed, and on countless other days when collective grief and anger poured through us, we needed to move with other people to address the magnitude of the trauma. We needed to heal together, to be with others who understood us—and part of that healing is getting through to the other side, regaining our collective agency, and making sure those things stop happening and that they won't ever happen to our children.

We get remade as we remake the world. When we build something together, relationship is created. Our fantasies of perfection or utopia are replaced with something I find more relieving and real, that we are alive and connected, that there is more to learn, that we change until our final moment, that we are both powerless at times and powerful. Engaging the world is about making our contribution, about exiting the safety of the sidelines and feeling the texture of deep practice and collective action. It is in that fray that we each become and that the world we shape responds to our needs. If ever there was a time to reactivate our tools for creation, if ever there was a time to elevate new stories of collaboration, it is now.

EXPANDING OUR WE

we are each other's
harvest:
we are each other's
business:
we are each other's
magnitude and bond.

—GWENDOLYN BROOKS,
"Paul Robeson"

MAYBE BEING A MIDDLE CHILD MAKES YOU MORE AWARE OF how tenuous belonging can be. Your version of parents is different from the version that was or will be. You do not have the striving parents of your older siblings or the permissive, applauding ones of the younger children. You have the parents who are already a little tired, who have not yet figured out that what makes them tired in part is the hypervigilance they will eventually abandon. It's easy for a middle child to internalize the story that they are too much or not enough. It's easy to feel out of place with your siblings, scrambling to keep up or always in the way. A middle child does not quite fit, has no authority that holds, is never innocent, and, being on the outside, is usually tasked with telling hard truths that no one wants to hear while struggling to make sure they can still belong once the words are spoken. I don't put much weight in birth order theory most of the time, as Black families, thankfully, complicate all of the research. We create the family structures we need. We have grandmothers who are second mothers, cousins who are more like siblings, and uncles our own age. We make family our own way. I wouldn't believe any of it had merit except the descriptions perfectly depict my life as a middle child. I had too much emotion, rocked the boat too often, was too insistent on being different. With the gauntlet of school added in, I had the recipe for a lifelong investigation into human belonging, into finding my place and my kin.

High school lunchtime was a survey in self-segregation. Black kids took up two tables near the window. The ends of those tables became the beginnings of the tables where Latiné kids sat. There was similarity there, laughter and music. Lunchtime at those tables was a respite and recharge. At the center were the monied kids, mostly white, who pulled out perfectly assembled lunches. The nerds sat at a table in the corner of the lunchroom, checking equations and showing off the games they'd programmed into their TI-83 calculators. Along the wall were the skater and emo kids who wore wide-legged jeans and makeup. I floated between tables, talking to everyone, then visiting the wall on my way to the library, where I always spent the second half of lunch reading books

to catch a glimpse of the world beyond our town. I had an ir-
reverence that made it easy for me to strike up a conversation
with anyone. I befriended kids in every group, moving back
and forth among them, not worried about the barriers that
people created between one another, fascinated instead by
everyone's stories, lives, and music tastes.

I was grappling with my sexuality during that time, so floating between groups was a way of protecting myself. I knew that
if I landed anywhere or stayed too long I would give people
the chance to possibly see me—and then reject me—and so I
never touched down. But from my vantage point, I could see
everyone else, equally odd and beautiful, the way we were all,
in our teenage awkwardness, living through the same sagas.
Fear of my own rejection made way for an unexpected generosity of spirit. On the other side of our differences, I could sense
that there were things common to us, interests and impulses,
shared tendencies, though some were flavored or remixed by
our own cultures. I could see people's essences—even if I
wasn't convinced that they would see mine.

As I grew older and queerer, my circles of belonging grew
smaller and smaller. Church preached that gayness was a sin,
made a big show of it on Sunday afternoons, as though loving
each other were killing Black people. I was terrified of anyone
finding out about me. I prayed to God to take the queerness
away and when it remained in the morning, I prayed for God
to take me in my sleep. My mother, no doubt shaped by this
same fear, went through my things looking for evidence of
my queerness and eventually found it. Soon after, she sent
me to a therapist who specialized in conversion. For most of
the session, the therapist prayed about how God loved me
but hated the evil spirit that had come to occupy my body. I

levitated above her and her incantations; my fear was the only thing converted. It distorted and split itself into an enduring shame and a simmering rage. All this time, I had feared that belonging could be retracted if I was honest about who I was. It was now confirmed to me that I could not belong anywhere as myself.

When something that seems innate is taken from you, the pain of its loss tells you its shape. I know viscerally how our bodies need belonging, what it is to crave it, and what it is to try to give up on it. I know the cruelty it is to withhold it. For those who are granted acceptance by protections bestowed by institutions and a culture that celebrates you, the need to belong might be more difficult to identify. It's a given, an entitlement for playing by the mostly arbitrary rules, rules that deny access and inclusion to any but the privileged few. But many of us on the edges know that belonging is survival, and when we don't have it, our very existence, our lives, are at risk.

Times are turbulent and unpredictable. No matter our affiliation or perspective, if we look soberly around, we can't help but see that the world is on the brink. We are exhausted, anxious, and agitated. At a time when we perhaps need one another the most, when the threats we face spare none of us, we are our most fractured. Motivated by the barrage of bad news and the fear that these ever-present crises won't end well, we've broken into factions to try to reverse the destruction or, for some, to accelerate it. Instead of turning toward one another to find collaboration and connection, we've calcified into the rhetoric of us versus them, creating sacrificial scapegoats from the most vulnerable, finding reasons for division and splintering along every aspect of human identity and relationship. Many of us have narrowed our visions and turned to protecting those we define as our own, our "we," reining in our ideas of who matters and who is deserving of our care. The justification, we say, is safety, but the method is often dehumanization and a denial of our interconnection that only makes us more vulnerable. If we are to meet this moment, it requires that we find our way to one another and risk confronting the past. That we acknowledge the harm done and do the challenging and rewarding work of learning to relate to one another in new ways, expanding our sense of who we are and who we are related to.

Belonging isn't an experience we can opt out of or live without. For our species, it's as necessary as the air we breathe. If the Covid-19 pandemic taught us anything, it is that we are all bound together in this life on earth, and our collective behaviors shape our continued existence here. We know that when a deadly virus breaks out, it can circle the globe and bring the world to its knees within weeks—and that our individual actions have important consequences for people we may never know. When millions of us banded together and suffered the inconvenience and stresses of multiple lockdowns, we slowed the spread of a disease and saved the lives of strangers. And yet, even then we could not erase the weight of history that meant that infection rates, deaths, and losses of all kinds landed more heavily on poor people and "essential" workers, and on disabled, Black, Brown, and Indigenous bodies. To move forward and heal as a society, we must confront and reckon with the facts that allow some of us to be more vulnerable to harm while many of us exist at the expense of others, imagining our lives as worth more, and hoarding power and resources to keep ourselves protected. To ensure our survival as a society, we must extend to everyone the safety and care we want for ourselves.

To belong is to rest into the collective, to be woven into the all. It's the feeling that the group has found meaning and usefulness in your presence. That what you bring is needed and wanted here. At the very least, it is to know that we are connected whether we like it or not. As James Baldwin wrote: "Each of us, helplessly and forever, contains the other—male in female, female in male, white in black and black in white. We are a part of each other. Many of my countrymen appear to find this fact exceedingly inconvenient and even unfair, and so, very often, do I. But none of us can do anything about it."

When we choose to deny that interconnection by othering, by seeing some of us as less worthy, we refuse to submit to a clear and urgent lesson from our universe: When we don't care for all of us, what is allowed to happen to me will eventually be done to you. The pathogen in my body will find its way into yours. Oppression manufactures and reinforces the idea that the "other" is irreconcilably and fundamentally different from us, is not one of us, to relieve us of any impulse toward consideration and care. It's true that difference, like relationship, is a fact. But difference itself is not a sound basis for denial of entry into any community that is concerned with its own thriving and adaptation. The director of the Othering & Belonging Institute at the University of California, Berkeley, john a. powell, has said, "The opposite of Othering is not 'saming,' it is belonging. And belonging does not insist that we are all the same. It means we recognise and celebrate our differences, in a society where 'we the people' includes all the people." Difference can be a resource, an expansion of our skills and perspectives. Our edges and gaps are the places where we can benefit from one another.

It makes a kind of sense that a society that exalts the individual, that extols independence, self-expression, and autonomy, would compromise the collective value of its people. This rigid and rugged individualism stems from one of our most central founding myths, that this country was created singularly by men who conquered the terrain and the uncivilized people who lived on it. These white men created and were promised a kind of freedom, allowed only to them, to pursue their visions, with little to no regulation or concern for the whole. On a societal level, this meant a contraction of care, excluding many to benefit the few. Because of this myopia, this hyperfocus on the individual, our culture has a hard time seeing in systems, seeing the interconnection between us. Human institutions and systems are made of individuals but take on a spirit and quality bigger than any one person can generate on their own. What we create ends up at some point creating us. It's how rigid inventions like race or gender can persist and evolve long after the original authors of these fictions are gone. Ghosts animate the machine. But our training and sense of ourselves as individual keep us from acknowledging that what came before lives in the foundation of our moment, keeps us from understanding what water we are swimming in, and how we create, mindlessly, a version of what already was.

A culture of individualism doesn't require us to consider that as our power grows, so too might our responsibility to others. Under its spell, we are accountable for just our one life and lifetime, able to act with the recklessness of a meteor, crashing through resources without concern for their renewability. We do not have the ability or incentive to see seven generations down the line as the Haudenosaunee nation instructs. Instead, we praise hoarding and greed, and make taking into an individual right, without expecting that we owe something to the people and social fabric that made us. Stories of how we did everything on our own, alone, the pioneer, are the only kind of stories individualism recognizes as legitimate. A story that is surely never true but conveys a triumph over circumstances and, too often, the people around us. To tell that story we have to deny our teachers, our supporters, the people who taught, fed, and loved us, the systems and history we navigated.

If we cannot bootstrap ourselves into dominance, we end up living alone. The child of individualism is isolation—and for social animals, isolation is deadly. It deteriorates our minds and bodies and creates health risks for the individual and danger for the group. There's vulnerability in being left behind. We can become prey, lured into the traps of ideologies that would use our bodies for their own purposes, to secure their own power. Mass shooters are always described as isolated, lone-wolf gunmen. It's hard to reconcile how common these stories have become with how alone the young men that commit them seem to be. It's their isolation and the vulnerability of it that connect them to one another. Their sense of disconnection has consequences for the whole.

The way we've set it up now, what is substituted for true belonging is proximity to power. There's no rest or reassurance in our belonging, no trust that what is innate to us is accepted. Instead, there's a grasping, an insecure scramble for the top. Belonging, as we know, can be retracted. Groups can be pitted against one another even though what they share is

more substantial than what separates them. People can easily be isolated or singled out, as we've seen with the increasingly unsettling attacks on gender nonconforming and trans
people. We can come to believe that the only way to secure
our rights is to undermine or threaten the other: the zero-sum
game. We protect who sits at the top of this unstable pyramid,
and stay focused on how to belong the way they do, forgetting
that we would build a stronger, wider power if we focused
on who was relegated to the bottom, who barely registers as
human in this society.

SOMETIME LAST YEAR, I WAS in conversation with a woman,
whom I think it is important to name as white, who'd recently
come out as lesbian. She asked me if one way to resolve injustice would be to sit down with people who might reject me because of race or sexuality and show them that I was, in the end,
just like them. It had worked with her own family, she said, her
explaining to them that she and her wife were normal, church-
going, taxpaying people. I told her I had few problems sitting
down with anyone, but the frame of her question was danger-
ously askew and offered up something of her—and my—soul
for barter. "Who in the end is more human than you or me that
we should plead for acceptance into their version of humanity?
I am not just like them and I am human still." We have been
told for so long now that difference makes us alien that we've
come to accept it and to grant other people the right to gate-
keep us, to make us ask for admission into their narrow concept
of who belongs, who is useful. Expanding our concept of "we"
is not about erasing difference but about redefining human to
include all of us for who we really are.

When Toni Morrison was seventeen, she saw footage on the news of a group of white mothers in the South trying to overturn a school bus filled with Black children on their way to integrate schools. It was shocking, baffling, to her how these mothers could threaten the lives of children, terrorize a bus full of other mothers' babies. She tried to understand their ruthlessness and depravity, what logic they used to justify it to themselves, and the only way she could come close to the fear and rage they seemed to feel was to look outside of our own species: "I said suppose . . . horses began to speak. And began to demand their rights. Now, I've ridden horses. They're very good workers. They're very good racehorses. Suppose they just . . . want more. Suppose they want to go to school! Suppose they want to sit next to me in the theatre. I began to feel this sense of—'I like you, but . . .'; 'You're good, but . . .' Suppose they want to sleep with my children?!" These women could not see their violence as irrational, morally impoverished acts against the most vulnerable of us because they had been so trained to see Black people as less than human, an adjacent and infiltrating species set apart.

Around 2014, I wrote a post on Facebook:

> It would be different if slavery were simply coercive employment. But in order for the system to work as well as it did, it relied on people understanding themselves as God surrogates and convincing others they were subhuman. These are massive psychological, emotional, and spiritual shifts that no policy could touch or change. We left slavery with no shared agenda on how we all find our way back to what is actually true. Instead, we've been passing down slightly reformed versions of this same per-

spective, lost in the confusion, with little sense of what needs to change. Slavery is not just an economic story. It's a story of how humanity can betray itself, it's the story of what destruction a lie can do, how people can be traumatized and terrorized out of their selves, and yet reshape what is truly humane, and how others must fall from the lie of innocence to become tender, listening, rooted, and human again.

Those women's actions against children on a school bus are a replication of this fundamental and seductive delusion, this negating of another person's humanity. It's mirrored in the rhetoric of the so-called Great Replacement theory, and we see it in mass shootings in churches and stores that Black and Brown people frequent and in Charlottesville in 2017 when white supremacists chanted, "You will not replace us." Who is the "us" that is facing replacement, I wonder, watching their reddened faces shrieking into the camera? Are they really afraid for their bodies or afraid for their place in society? Do they know but won't admit that it's their use of violence and domination whose time has actually come? That their bodies are not being asked to die, only their practices of othering and exclusion that deny our connection, our shared humanity?

As horrific as these acts are, as terrifying as their consequences have been across time, they are the acts of the small-hearted, the fearfully cruel. They are not the courageous acts of people who can build futures, but eruptions of the basest of human tendencies and an immature fear of the dark that attempts to turn difference into monstrosities it can defeat. This tendency to dehumanize betrays an underdevelopment, an overidentification with a flimsy self-concept. It is a contraction we hold in society that says safety can only be granted for some.

From the beginning of Black Lives Matter, in a departure from past iterations of Black movement, the declaration has been that All Black Lives matter. The signal there was that we need to work as hard to end violence against Black women and girls, trans women, and gender nonconforming people as we do the unjust, brutal murders of Black men. Rekia Boyd. Toyin Salau. Breonna Taylor. Atatiana Jefferson. Sandra Bland. Ma'Khia Bryant. Their lives matter no less. The hard truth is that many of those who violate women and queer people are in fact the Black men who are said to love them or at least desire them. Black people have not been immune to these small, fearful rankings of people, to subjugating the feminine, to fearing the dark in us. It's a painful contradiction, but one that is worth telling the truth about. We can deny full humanity even to those to whom we are closely related and expected to care for. The mirror often scares us. When a Black trans woman is assaulted in her own community because her insistence on her own life reflects to some men the constraints they apply to their own bodies and emotions, their violence toward her is a violence toward the part of themselves that is also soft and beautiful. It splinters their own interiors into a million isolated others. The need for reckoning and reformation goes deep.

Our definition of human and whom we allow to belong has to be brought down from its perch of exclusivity, disassembled, and reimagined. We need to remove the imposed stratifications and hierarchies. I choose to redefine humanity on terms bigger than my own reflection or my own comfort. Humanity is varied, changing, a species capable of great beauty and destruction, struggling to feel all that we are capable of—love, for example, and the fear and reality of our death. A species still barely known to itself, barely willing to call one another by name, and still only beginning to encounter the magnitude of being alive at all. What is it possible for a human to be? What is shared between us beyond phenotypes or regions? When we have been trained or traumatized into a warped belonging, we might think that the only way we can belong is to control the bodies of the people around us, or we might have come to believe that belonging means that we have to hide our bodies and feeling away. None of this is the kind of belonging that settles us or sets us free. Instead, we need to practice new ways of connecting and ways of creating relationship that are strange and beautiful.

KIN

EVERY SUNDAY NIGHT AT MY HOUSE we have family dinner: my partner, Kasha; our kid, Amaya; and Denise, a dear friend whom I've known for a decade. Last year, we convinced Denise to move near to us from where she was living in Florida because when we're together it's such an easy, fun time. A couple of years ago, she mentioned that she was starting to think about who she wanted to be close to as she got older. She doesn't have children, though she has loved and nurtured so many people in Black movement. Kasha and I both, if we're honest, need intergenerational relationships, need the wisdom and dad jokes of someone older than us, and we wanted our child to grow up around someone who balances sweetness and conviction the way Denise does. "Denise," I'd said, "come here and we'll take care of each other. We want to make family with you." When the Covid-19 pandemic hit, it seemed as good a time as any to start creating the kind of kin we needed.

Every Sunday, Denise brings her dog Bandit, a love child of our dog Scout and a rambling Doberman who broke into our yard, and sibling to our Little Bear. Each household takes turns preparing the meal. It's often the most elaborate one I have each week. Over food we share our exciting news, our heartaches, too, and our assessments of the state of the union. This gathering is our safe harbor in the midst of many storms, where we can be both petty and profound, where we laugh and confess and remember what it is to belong in someone's care. I have been elected to say our grace, so before each meal I say a prayer that usually ends with something like "Thank you to the force that is greater than us, to our creator, for this opportunity to intentionally make a family out of love." At the end of the meal, Denise helps us clean up and we put Amaya to bed. The dogs cuddle in theirs and we talk on the couch or sit in the hot tub until we are sleepy, too. All of this is part of the ritual that binds us, this family we've made.

No one teaches us how to build a family, how to decide that people with whom we share no blood are relatives. We know somehow that romantic love can do it, can fuse our lives to another person's, but it's a magic we're told is reserved for the one. Queerness says different. The story of the outcast, the expelled, if they survive, is often the story of love in unforeseen places. Family forged in unconventional and peculiar ways. People taking care of one another, making someone who was a stranger our very own business. Abandonment can push us to admit what others often won't: We all need one another to survive, and it is our insistence on narrowing our care and concern, on throwing away those we treat as other, that jeopardizes our ability as humans, as societies, to flourish.

Writer and scholar Donna Haraway talks about the need to create other and new bonds to face our difficult times, saying, "Staying with the trouble means making oddkin; that is, we require each other in unexpected collaborations and combinations, in hot compost piles. We become—with each other or not at all." "This kinship," she has said, "is reciprocal and non-optional, that if you have a kin, a kin has you." Oddkin, chosen family, strange and beautiful affiliations, open up new pathways of relationship and social formations—and may be exactly what we need right now to survive.

Practicing kinship is looking into one another's faces and admitting that we are familiar and related. It's rejecting the fear that there is not enough care for all of us, an unfortunate illusion created by our current systems and culture in which separation from and by one another produces the perception and reality of scarcity. Instead, kinship creates the abundance we need.

Who do we care about, and how are we willing to care about them? Who are we responsible for? When we ask ourselves these questions, we can begin to move beyond narrow concepts to expand our sense of "we" by extending our care beyond the confines of what we've been taught, and to expand our bodies to be able to live with the complexity and complication of what another person's perspective and life may reveal to us. This expansion is an orientation more than a goal, and it happens in the dangerous terrain of intimacy, of connection made possible through the skills of authenticity, setting boundaries, and trust, both as embodied skills and as

felt capacities. It is both a feeling and a way of being transformed by a reality we can only encounter through another:
an embodied joining, a true connection.

EMPATHY

MAKING ODDKIN, FINDING KIN IN other people, requires that
we know empathy and that the cultures we create reinforce
it. Empathy, the capacity to understand and feel what another
person is experiencing, is one of the first things you learn
about when becoming a therapist. It's key to the therapeutic
alliance, the kind of relationship that makes it possible for
someone to feel safe enough to be vulnerable. It is not as easy
as it sounds. In my first few sessions as a therapist, I wanted
more than anything to be useful to the people who came to
see me and to be good at what I was doing. So when they presented their problems, I scrambled for quick fixes, defined answers to their questions. I knew that when in doubt the thing
to do was to listen more deeply, but instead I found myself
giving advice or pointing out a pattern of behavior my client
seemed to be unconsciously laying out in front of me. After a
while, I took my anxieties to my supervisor, who explained to
me that empathy was a way of being with another person and
allowing what they are holding to touch you. That empathy
has the power to create a sense of safety for people in their
own emotions or experience—especially for someone being
received for the first time just as they are. I had wanted to fix,
I discovered, not only to relieve them of their troubles but also
to lift myself out of the chaos, out of my own insecurity and
fear that the feeling would rub off on me. Empathy is something much more vulnerable. Fixing, after all, is just another

way to stop feeling. With empathy I found more feeling, not less. More connection, not less. I could sit with the people I worked with and let their experience affect me. I could have enough curiosity to consider what it meant to them, not just how I might react to it.

Empathy is distinct from sympathy, which is protective at its root. Sympathy is offered from a safe distance. It's often a performative "I'm sorry that happened," without being willing to feel any of it. Sympathy is handed down from on high. Empathy also isn't the kind of guilt that confuses us into believing that if we feel badly enough something will change. It won't. What really changes things are our connections, meaningful relationships, and the actions we take on together to create something new.

The thing about empathy is that most of the time it comes when we stop trying to do anything and allow ourselves to actually listen and feel. A lot of times we resist letting in someone else's pain. But if we are unwilling to feel for someone in their grief, we are, in essence, unwilling to know them and know ourselves. And if we are unwilling to know someone, if we'd rather keep a safe distance through sympathy or apathy, we likely won't know how to have their back when it counts.

Empathizing is the embodied act of widening our sphere of care. In the folds of empathy lie both longing and curiosity. Longing is the full-bodied pull toward another person or to a future, and curiosity is an openness to learning what we don't yet know, that by its very nature may cause us to feel or change. To be empathetic means that we allow ourselves to be impacted by another without merging with them, by maintaining our own center in the connection. It can take a kind of internal safety to be curious, to stay steady as relationship opens itself to us and shows us things we didn't know. Empathy is listening with an open chest that allows us to understand.

ALLYSHIPS AND ACCOMPLICES

I WAS TEMPTED TO PROVIDE a checklist of tasks and tips on how to be a great ally or accomplice in the fight for justice, but any lists you need have already been written. And to be honest, I believe they provide cover for the deeper transformation, the fundamental change that is necessary for their advice to stick. We don't really change on account of good ideas, no matter how much we may wish to, or because we hope to be perceived as politically correct, or even because we truly want to find a way to make things better. Instead, we change because we have surrendered with our bodies to feeling something new, to expanding our capacity to experience a wider range of emotions, to deepen relationships, and to open our awareness.

I was really changed recently by something Kasha said to me in a conversation about allyship—which was that we must first be able to feel grief, our own, before we can truly become an ally to anyone else. We have to know what it is to have lost. For all of us striving to achieve, climbing the ladders of success or acceptance in our society, that might well mean we have to stop and admit that there's something that we've given up to play the game. There are things worth grieving that have been taken from all of us. Knowledge about the ecosystem that we're a part of, the ability to be vulnerable and intimate with one another, the resilience practices of our ancestors, reverence for the great mystery of it all. When we don't know our own grief, we aren't able to really listen when someone tells us what they've lost or are losing or what has been taken from them, perhaps for our benefit. We aren't able to show up for anyone else because we've disallowed the power and connection that are possible when we feel.

I've needed this kind of allyship with people around gender. I've done so many Gender 101 trainings for organizations, but none of them ever hit home until I showed people that gender is not something that only queer people are afflicted with, that gender is an experience all of us are navigating at any point in time. We're all making assessments about how we present, and most of us feel some insecurity at not meeting the standards set out for us. Are we pretty enough, strong enough, tall enough, jaws chiseled enough, waists thin enough to be real?

Allyship, though, is not about flattening our experiences. We are not all going through the same things, and some people are more explicitly punished for their difference, some are feeling the pain more acutely and alone. This is true, but cultivating an empathy that allows another person under your skin is the beginning of building meaningful and real connections and trust.

We retrieve some of our humanness through feeling our own hurt and only then can we sit with the reality of another's grief and pain. All of us, every people, have a history with pain. It is how we find one another through our varied stories and bodies. If we skip that step for our own safety and comfort, or if we opt for guilt that keeps us from feeling our own loss and despair, guilt that keeps us safe on a pedestal, there will come a point when we turn around, a moment when we will not have the courage to do what is needed, because we won't yet know that as we fight for another's life we are fighting for our own.

Allyship is not just something we think we are or can do. It requires our bodies to feel, to develop, and to experience empathy, and to take action and risks where appropriate. Allyship requires each of us to begin to put our bodies in new places, sometimes in front of people who would be picked off, sometimes having the backs of people who can lead us into places we haven't gone, the same people we have been trained to be glad we are not.

There are no saviors in a circle, no heroes, just people taking risks for a vision of another way. There is more evidence for this kind of solidarity than we are told about. In fact, I would guess that it would be impossible to study any movement, any people's struggle toward freedom, and not find, somewhere along the edges, that empathy inspired people who were not in the crosshairs to become allies and join their fight. In recent years, cross-racial organizing by Asians 4 Black Lives has demanded an end to state violence and anti-Black sentiment in their own communities, multi-faith actions called for an end to Trump's so-called Muslim bans, and after a series of anti-Asian hate crimes people from different communities rallied across the country to condemn the violence and show support for Asian Americans. These are all examples of allyship that we can learn from.

BELONG TO EARTH

WHEN NO ONE ELSE HAD ME, it was the ground that held my feet. When I felt my most insecure or unwanted, I always knew how to get lost. In the depth of the forest, the movement of the creek. I can tell by how my attention settles that I belong here, if nowhere else. That I am from and of this ecosystem. It's a belonging I haven't had to doubt. When we feel alone, it can be helpful to be with the life around us that has remained here whether or not we see or acknowledge it. Microbes and insects, birds and trees that are regenerating, adapting, restoring. When we look for models of allyship, we can learn from the steadiness of the earth beneath our feet. It has always been here, living alongside us, but recently many of us have moved away from it, grown separate, and stopped caring. We extract from this earth that nourishes us without replenishing; we encroach upon it, trampling land and creatures without acknowledgment or restoration. We no longer see the people who grow our food, or know where it comes from, and we don't eat according to the seasons. This separation has allowed us to strain the environment in which we live in ways that threaten our survival and the survival of other life in our ecosystem. Climate change is showing us the impacts of our deep disconnection, of not feeling a sense of belonging to earth.

While there is no map showing us how we get out of this confusing story, I believe it will require us falling back in love with the complex ecosystem that creates and sustains us. As scientist and author Robin Wall Kimmerer says, "We need acts of restoration, not only for polluted waters and degraded lands, but also for our relationship to the world." And for our relationship to one another by fighting for a different way of life based on reciprocity and renewal. It is the role of transitional characters, the people willing to take on the work of transformation in their spheres of care and influence, to move away from the narrowing and isolating trends of this time and to build authentic community with one another in all our vast humanity, one that ultimately creates more safety for everyone.

Last summer, I led a beautiful embodiment training that turned into a celebration of divinity. On the last night, the participants headed to the pool and I stopped in to say my goodbyes. One person called me over to the edge and said, "Did you notice how everyone is floating in a perfect circle? Every time someone joins, a space just opens up without anybody saying anything. The first night we came to the pool we were all over the place, and tonight it's like we've become our own organism."

There is almost nothing more profound or more terrifying than the simple act of reaching for each other. There is no real intimacy that does not begin with listening. And there is no chance that we can show up for each other if one or both of us is still somehow an object. The task ahead of us is hard, to weave a belonging between people who have never belonged to one another or have forgotten what it is to accept and invite. To fold ourselves back into earth, as creatures of it and not above it. It's hard because of how many barriers we've built between us. But like so many things that seem difficult at first, to start the work of belonging is deceivingly uncomplicated. It is putting aside, in this moment, the stories we tell, not of difference, but of inherent and complete separation. We are already kin, whether we like it or not. So how can we live as though our living depends on one another?

7

THINGS FALL APART

I know the world is bruised and bleeding, and though it is
important not to ignore its pain, it is also critical to refuse
to succumb to its malevolence. Like failure, chaos contains
information that can lead to knowledge—even wisdom.

—Toni Morrison,
"No Place for Self-Pity, No Room for Fear"

AT THE END OF 2017 I HAD A HEALTH SCARE. AT THE TIME, I WAS
on staff at Black Lives Matter Global Network, and we were
at the height of crisis. In fact, we'd spent most of our time
that year responding to crises: ongoing police violence, pressure from the media, threats from the right, and challenges
that originated inside the organization—disagreements, mis-
understandings, and mistrust. Working there, we were trying
to build something bigger than anything we'd ever seen, trying
to keep something together that was probably too big to be
contained. It felt like trying to harness the wind.

A week earlier I had been to the funeral of a friend's partner, a Black woman just a handful of years ahead of me in her forties. She'd died suddenly, tragically, from heart failure. A beloved chef, she had cooked for everyone's retreats, weddings, and fundraisers, and the outpouring of love and grief shown in return was beautiful and profound. At her funeral I quietly promised myself I'd make an appointment to see the doctor. I'd had chest pains for the last month that had begun to trouble me. When I was facilitating conflicts or on late-night emergency phone calls, my chest would tighten and radiate like a violent sunburst coming from my heart. Despite all my training as a bodyworker, despite knowing better, I'd grit my teeth and try to ignore it until the wave passed. I believed, as we all did, that what we were doing at BLM was contributing to our freedom. That to get there we just had to endure these immediate challenges, the internal disagreements, and the external barrage of threats. As one of the organization's healing practitioners, I thought that if I could find enough compassion in me, could open my heart wide enough to consume some of the pain and rage we all felt and directed toward ourselves and one another, we might then find a way to stay together, to trust one another enough to disrupt the systems that seemed hell-bent on killing us. But sitting at the funeral, tears in my eyes, hearing stories about our friend's life and the grief her absence opened up, I knew that I needed to pay attention to the pain in my chest. That my body was communicating to me about my limits. I was being asked to listen even if part of me was afraid to hear what my body was saying.

The next week I found myself at the doctor's office, sitting on the edge of an examination table explaining those pains and shortness of breath to the nurse. If I'm honest, I only half listened to her, watching out of the corner of my eye as my phone lit up with messages from our organization's text thread. An incident there was escalating, and we were all struggling to determine what to do and how to respond. I was searching for a solution that would settle things down. Even as a doctor hooked me up to an EKG machine, I was frantically, though apologetically, texting with my colleagues. It was only when the doctor returned with a clipboard and a worried look that I put down my phone. She sat across from me and with one of those weighted doctor tones asked me again to describe the pain I'd felt. "Have you been experiencing any more stress than usual?" she asked. "I feel stress constantly," I answered, stone-faced. "Well," she said, "the EKG results show that you've had a heart incident." "What does that mean?" I asked, suddenly starting to wish I'd taken Kasha up on her offer to come with me. "It could have been an injury, some kind of blunt force to your heart," the doctor said with a tone of regret. "Or a small heart attack." I was thirty-six and terrified.

The immediate prescription was time off from work and further testing. I spent most of the next few weeks at home resting, staying away from my phone. Lying down, I could hear the adrenaline coursing through me still, whirring in my ears. I startled easily, found myself worked up over minor things, agitated, playing out worst-case scenarios in my mind. I was detoxing from all the stress I had been operating under. I started seeing an acupuncturist as often as she would take me. The first time there I lay stomach down, a million needles bristling in my back, and ugly-cried into the face hole of the table. I decided right then that I needed to leave the organization and stop working for as long as we could afford. I had been going so hard, trying to respond to internal and exter-

nal conflicts, trying to keep everything and everyone together,
that I hadn't listened to the warning signs of my own body. I
hadn't remembered that everything we experience is experienced in our bodies, that stress exacts a toll that is, too often,
collected from our organs and life spans. I had also missed
one of my own key facilitation points, that conflict is a teacher
we would do better to listen to. In wanting to stop all conflicts
from happening and make sure everyone else was okay, I had
become a victim of my attempts to keep the peace.

The law of entropy tells us that everything eventually falls
apart. Despite our best efforts, our good intentions, and how
much we've healed, whatever we build—our relationships,
our organizations, our families, even the society we have come
to know—can and will break down. What we assume is or-
dered will become disordered. Some moments in history are
rife with conflicts. This is one of them. Not only are we having
conflict, but conflict, it seems, is having us. Grinding us up
and spitting us out, disconnected, demoralized, and enraged.
On a societal level, conflict is teaching us a lesson we have
not yet figured out how to learn. That sometimes we would do
better to allow crises to destabilize us, to accept them and
listen to them more, or at the very least not resist them so
fervently. Instead, most of us do what I did. When we find
ourselves in conflict, we fight against it in the name of maintaining some flimsy version of control over the situation. We
do everything we can to protect ourselves, to identify and defend against the other side that has solidified around our disagreements. We fight until we feel sufficiently right, or good,
or until we have exhausted the other, or we run to find the
nearest exit. But what seems to be true is that conflict does
not disappear just because we want it to or because we hide it

away. When we choose not to deal with it, it can remain alive in our relationships and in societies, an acidifying, molten undercurrent waiting to erupt.

We can have unresolved conflicts from childhood, a box of crayons stolen by a sibling, that anger us far into adulthood. And we can live in suppressed and unresolved societal conflicts that remain intractable for hundreds of years. Conflict sticks around until we get it. And when we do, it offers us an opportunity. In thousands of hours of facilitating conflict over the years, I have come to understand that every conflict holds something, a message, a lesson, for us. Inside of every conflict is something that we can use—but most of us never fully realize this, especially when we're caught up in the heat of discord. This is not to say that everything we do in conflicts is justified, just that their existence is an opportunity to learn something new, if we know how to find it, about ourselves, one another, and the world.

I wonder if we think we know about conflict already because we consume it all the time. We entertain ourselves with fights. The sports we play and watch are skillful, rule-bound conflicts in action, and the plotlines of many reality TV shows depict wealthy people in perpetual disagreement assaulting one another at dinner parties. Our national politics and our engagement with it are some of our least skillful displays of conflict, as evidenced by comments sections all over the internet, dumpster fires of regurgitated and vitriolic talking points. Conflict is everywhere but rarely do we see examples of it doing anything other than intending and causing destruction and pain.

This nonstop consumption of conflict is a by-product of the collective anxiety we feel as we face uncertain and high-stakes futures. Escalating climate change and technological and political tensions heighten every collective decision we must make. Paradoxically, conflict entertainment is a distraction from these decisions and from deep, sustained engagement with our shared issues. It might be that we try to trap conflict in our screens, entertaining ourselves with others' misfortunes because we are trying, as I was, to keep conflict under control. But pretending that conflict is only entertainment just underprepares us for its inevitable arrival in our own lives.

Malidoma Patrice Somé, the late spiritual teacher and author, once said of conflict that it is the nature of a relationship asking to deepen. I find this to be so true. It is a natural part of any living system. It's one of the ways we discover together our differences in belief, approach, and needs. It can help us move from one stage to the next. Just as the seedling pushes against its casing. The teenager argues for freedom. A couple begins to disagree over the smallest things after having a child. Relationships show their edges and change. Conflict isn't an anomaly or a personal failure, nor is it an indication that a relationship is bad at its core. It is mostly the surfacing of the unconscious, what we don't yet know, and what we've suppressed. We can expect it to arise whenever people come together to try to do anything at all, as our needs and interests will and do brush up against one another's. It's as common to our personal relationships as it is to our work in the world. What's understood as allyship is often being willing to step into conflicts that we may have otherwise avoided or not noticed. Conflict is not only natural to us; it's needed for change.

When our team at the Embodiment Institute hosts healing retreats, we often joke that the third day of any course is "conflict day." On the first day, everyone is too nervous and protected to be anything but polite. By the second day, people are comfortable enough with one another to start to self-reflect, to feel scary new feelings. And the third day is when people start to bump up against one another. When they take the risk to say what they really feel, or try to interrupt their people-pleasing tendencies. It can start to feel like a family gathering once the niceties have fallen away. Inevitably, the results are conflicts of all sizes. How we move through them together shows people how possible it is to have conflicts in their own lives, perhaps their own families, and to stay in relationship. That the two can exist together. It's a learning for all of us in making room for the unplanned.

WHEN I LEFT BLM, I took some much-needed time off to rest and recover and, honestly, to grieve. The cardiology tests were, in the end, inconclusive, though I knew with some certainty that my heart had been broken somewhere along the way. I cried every day over what I saw as my failures and missteps and the mistakes I'd seen from others. But as I came to terms with what had happened I was able to see the lessons more clearly. Lying in bed, I dissected and put back together every single breakdown I'd been a part of, facilitated, or witnessed. I read books and listened to talks from mediators and facilitators who worked on international conflict and war, wanting to understand why conflict could go so quickly from an opening to an impasse, one that could take years for people and organizations to recover from. What were the factors that created conflict, and what contributed to them feeling so intractable? Over the years, I have seen conflict tear people apart and dissolve the work they had intended to do. But, on occasion, I've also seen conflict bring people closer together, strengthen what they were trying to build. What were these moments of revelation and honest connection inside conflict made of? How had we created them? What made one conflict genera-tive, moving us toward understanding, and another caustic? How could we engage in conflict while minimizing the harm it could bring? What did we need to know and do to get to the other side?

Early on in my career doing couples therapy, I learned something that I came to see as a theme of generative con-flict. At first, when I asked a couple why they had come in, they started to show their conflict dance to me: how they each saw the conflict, how they defended themselves in it, and how they reinterpreted the incident to protect themselves. They described their issue, some painstakingly, as though more de-tails would naturally cause me to acquit them and convict their partner. And their partner was always at fault. *I only get pissed off because of what she does. He stays on his phone all day. They make me feel like I don't matter.* I listened to their accusa-tions. What were they really trying to say, and what were they really trying *not* to say? I'd offer their words back to them, re-stating what I'd heard in a way that defanged their statement. I'd try, "So what I hear you saying is that you are worried that she doesn't desire you anymore?" Or "Are you saying that you need more space? It also sounds like maybe some resentment has been growing because you've had to put their needs be-fore your own? Is that close?" Often, they'd return a relieved yes when they felt resonance, and most times, though not every time, their partner would drop their shoulders or offer, "I didn't know you felt like that." There is always something that we are most afraid of saying, the truth we protect at all costs. For interpersonal conflict to be productive, the key is finding this dangerous truth and creating enough safety that people can be vulnerable enough to say it.

I sometimes think about conflict like this: At the very center is a gem, or, like in a video game, a set of wings or special shoes that make it easier to get where we have to go next. A prize that can only be retrieved by doing the very thing we feel least compelled to do, the thing that may not even occur to us as a viable option when we are in the eye of the storm. We can only win that very special, very needed gift when we allow ourselves to be vulnerable, despite the threat we feel. When we say what's truest for us, often whatever it is that makes us feel small, afraid, and as though we've relinquished the control we thought was holding everything together. If, in conflict, we're able to listen from a relaxed and undefended body to what is being shared and reflected back to us, then something alchemizes. We're given access to our learning then, when we can reveal the wound that needs to be addressed.

Sometimes we resist the lesson, and we're haunted instead by past traumas retelling an old story in new circumstances. Very often we move into old ways of operating, protecting ourselves from perceived threats or danger. We can get stuck in time until we can learn and receive what is trying to make itself understood. For my own sake, I wish it were different, that we could stay defended and still get the message. No one has tried to avoid opening up more than me. But in all the conflicts I've been in and around, I've never seen anyone get their lesson out of conflict without offering a little something they were afraid to give in return.

A couple of years ago, I was asked to facilitate a gathering for an organization, with regional chapters meeting together to devise their strategy. At one point I asked the room to divide into regions so that they could compile their victories and challenges and share back with the larger group. After most groups had gone off with their rolls of butcher paper, I noticed a gathering in the corner where people seemed distressed. A member broke off and came up to me. "Um, we're having a problem in the Midwest." I took a breath and headed over.

As soon as I walked up, I saw that it was not exactly one group, but two camps split, each orbiting around an angry person in the center. I'll call them Vickie and Bea. Lines had been drawn, and each side mumbled accusations. The women in the center mirrored each other, doing their best to look both disgusted and unbothered. I took each woman to one side and asked them to tell me the story of how we'd gotten to that moment. It turned out Vickie was angry that earlier in the retreat Bea had publicly criticized her and not privately pulled her aside. Bea was upset that Vickie had dropped the ball significantly at work and left others to pick up her slack. They were caught in a cycle of blame. I sat everyone down, shared the story back as I had come to hear it, taking care to connect with them while I spoke, creating a bridge between them even as they sat across the table scowling.

"A couple things stood out to me that I want to reflect back to you both. What I heard from Vickie was that you, Bea, are her mentor, and bringing feedback to the large group embarrassed her." Bea started to explain Vickie's mistake at work before I interrupted. I promised we would get to that, asked that she trust me to return to it. I wanted first for Vickie to explain how she saw Bea. Vickie's tough exterior started to melt, and her voice trembled. "I never had a mentor before.

I've just been on my own, but she took interest in me. She's so smart that she made me feel like I was worth something for the first time. I wanted her to be proud." Looking over, I saw tears had started to fill Bea's eyes, too. "What are you feeling now?" I asked. "I see myself in her," said Bea. "It's like looking in a mirror. I've been hard on her because being hard on myself was how I got here."

Suddenly air entered the room, jaws relaxed, and much-needed words were spoken. I asked Vickie about the work she had promised. "To be honest," she said, "I didn't know how to do it. I felt dumb, like it was proof I shouldn't be here. So I just hid." "What's your responsibility to this mentorship relationship?" I asked. "What's your part?" "I guess to ask for help when I need it," Vickie offered. We spent the next half hour creating some structure to their mentorship, some agreements and some timelines for improvement for them both. At the end they embraced deeply. Both had learned more about what they were hiding, the insecurities it brought up in them to need and be needed by each other. Their self-protection kept them from growing, kept them from clarity on what was working and what wasn't. It kept them from retrieving what was positive and useful in the conflict that they could put into action to deepen and develop their relationship.

We can tell so many stories of the benefits of being vulnerable, but there are good reasons why we don't start there or that we don't get there at all. For one, vulnerability feels and can be dangerous. It exposes us, our fears and our desires, to other people. Sometimes the people we are in conflict with aren't safe, and sometimes we assume that no one is. That shaky feeling we get when we ask for help or step up out of hiding and into leadership is our bodies' warning that we are entering new and unfamiliar terrain and we are not sure how to stay protected.

Most of us struggle to admit when we're scared, and a good number of us are scared most of the time.

That fear we carry, the fear that we have gotten so accustomed to that we no longer recognize it as baggage from the past, enlarges and inflames the content of every conflict. When I live most of the time afraid for my life, your oversight, our misunderstanding, can very easily feel like imminent death, even if it is not. For a long time, I identified as strong. I could remain outwardly poised under tremendous amounts of pressure. I could keep things moving despite being tired or demoralized. I could take on others' emotional needs without breaking down around my own. The tropes of the strong Black woman and man are a story we tell ourselves that comes directly from realizing that somehow we are still here after centuries of oppression. It's a way to recover some of our dignity after generations of violence, humiliation, and fear. But the cover, the hardening, that we call strength is not just evidence of our survival. It also disguises a terror that comes from knowing that many people have not survived and that there is an unresolved cruelty growing just below the crust of our society. We are afraid to be caught off guard, to be exposed, but that same fear keeps us from being known and from moving through conflict.

This fear, grounded as it is, does not preclude the truth that vulnerability is the portal through which conflict is transformed and transforms us. Fear is the reminder that our lives are precious and precarious. We hurt, we crave to be seen, valued, we despair and need one another, and we need separation sometimes, too. We are vulnerable in these lives. But we struggle to say these truths in conflict. They show how soft we are underneath our defenses. Instead, conflicts escalate because our armor prevents us from sharing these feelings that make us feel small and exposed or because another's armor tells us it is unsafe to do so. In conflicts, we believe it's risky to lay down our protection knowing that in that moment of vulnerability we can be hurt and disappointed, but there's risk, too, in not being vulnerable, in knowing that there is no way through the conflict to the lesson without it.

Sometimes we wrap our tender fears in judgments and in blame, punishing someone for making us bare our chests, holding tight the apologies that are ours to say until the other person shows they are worthy by apologizing first. We try to make people feel the pain we've felt, though we know somewhere in us that vengeance makes us insatiable. Another's pain can never relieve our own. Other times, we use shaming as our primary emotional tool. But shame impedes change. It just does. I know the fear and powerlessness that cause us to use it with one another, but that doesn't make it effective. "Let's put trying to make them feel bad aside for a second," I'll say to couples. "Say what it is that you feel. Say what you need. Say what you are afraid to say. I'll be here with you." When we share our fears and concerns, when we are vulnerable, that is when we make it possible for the longing inside our conflict to be known and satisfied, or at least we find out if it can be.

WHENEVER I'M IN CONFLICT, and I have been in my fair share, it makes me, my body, suddenly unpredictable. I am shaking, hot, there's an energy and movement in me that I feel is pumping, preparing me to do things that most times I'd rather not. At work, more times than I can count, when I'm facilitating a particularly intense moment, someone will look up at me almost pleadingly to confess, "I don't know why I'm crying." Or "I need to get out of here before I lose my shit." Conflict has a way of undoing us, of stretching us beyond our contained bodies, the shape that we usually identify with and feel safe in. Any pretense we may still hold that we are civilized, purely intellectual beings, above animal emotion, is threatened by the wild and desperate responses in our bodies when we are accused, dismissed, or challenged. It is uncomfortable to feel the range of emotions that exist when we are in conflict. But we can't leave the body or the feeling out. They are our guides.

We already know that our bodies know how to defend. For example, when reading this you may have the ability to distinguish between an argument with your friend who is not showing up for you in a breakup and a life-or-death situation, but in the midst of that real-life scenario, when your friend lets you down, your body may register their behavior as abandonment and act in all the ways we might when we are afraid that we are being left behind to die. In conflicts our survival instincts get activated. It serves us to know this as we navigate crises, rather than to pretend that our bodies and emotions are not part of the equation. We can learn how to feel and listen to our bodies' reactions without acting them out or becoming them.

We can let the emotion inhabit us, inflame us, and ask it, What are you protecting? What are you most afraid of? What do you need me to know? This encourages our bodies to show us what is at stake, how they are choosing protection, and helps us to act accordingly. Maybe we're in a situation we should leave rather than try to make it work. Or maybe it's worth taking a break so that we can return more processed through our own feeling and more capable of truly listening. More often than not, when we create safety for ourselves just by listening, our bodies will offer up our truth.

We might find in our inquiry into our bodies' reactions that we are afraid that this conflict is just like another we barely survived. That some of the charge of the past animates the present. Often the scale of our reaction and how imminently we perceive the threat directly correlate to how much residue we hold from the past and how much or how little healing we've done. Our past can maintain a hold on us that amplifies slights and misattunements, that judges events as crises even when they are not. When we know this, we can be curious about how much of an emotion we feel belongs to this time, to this conflict, and how much comes from another time. This can help us focus on the issue at hand while letting us see that we have other emotions that need to be processed through a different route.

Conflict can make us very unsure, and a body threatened craves certainty. This can affect the way we respond. I remember an argument from years ago when a girlfriend asked why I kept comparing her to people in my past. I'd start sentences with "I know what you're going to say because everyone always . . ." "Hey," she'd say, "you're not dealing with whoever that is right now. We have never gone down this road together." That simple reframe changed my practice; somehow, it made me feel safer in the unknown of conflict. Why project outcomes when instead I could see what was possible in this configuration, this time? When we're in those heightened states of reactivity, we often need the world to become black-and-white, binary, good and bad, so that we can move and defend decisively. So that we can state our position clearly, draw our line in the sand. But nuance lives in feeling; it lives in the body. And when we are able to hold and explore nuance in a situation, it leads to more precise actions. We see that contradictions can exist alongside one another, and we can hear and take in other perspectives. We can hold multiple motivations and truths in our core and live with that stewing of complexity until the next right action shows itself to us.

Frequently, we come to conflict more concerned with who is innocent or guilty than with what happened, what we need to understand, and what needs repair and attention. I get asked to facilitate people through conflict, help them find a way to agreements and understanding. I find that when the process starts, people plead to me as if I were a judge, trying to make the case for their innocence and the other party's guilt. Innocence is safety while guilt leaves them at risk for expulsion and isolation. Neither innocence nor guilt can describe a person, as they are not identity traits or accurate descriptors of who we are in relationship, and yet we treat them that way. Many times, as I've supported people in wading through hard feelings, hurt feelings, I've found that they are not grasping for understanding, but for the safety of innocence. For an independent party to give them reprieve so that they don't have to look further, feel more, or understand themselves. We do everything we can to avoid being charged as guilty—we stretch truths, obscure intentions, omit information, and build alliances to prevent any perception of culpability, none of which gets to the cause of the conflict or the possible ways through.

At the foundation of this innocence/guilt binary lies a simple belief that we cling to, that the world divides itself neatly into good and evil, though it is on us to discern who fits into which category. In an attempt to do so, we simplify our world, make a lazy sense of it, taking shortcuts with good and evil and assigning them identities and characteristics. We assume that some people are good while others are predisposed toward an indomitable badness, with history playing an important role in these assumptions. Colonization, for example, codified whiteness, maleness, and able-bodied Christians as the standard of goodness, rightness, and the way people should be in a civilized society. This story set those with these so-called attributes against the indistinct dark masses. The darker you are, the closer you are to nature, the more dangerous, the more criminal, the worse you can be assumed to be. The binary is fixated on reinforcing itself, so it disappears the existence of the so-called middle, the people who don't fit in either predetermined category. And the binary misses what is complex in each of us.

Innocence, as our society uses it, is not a concept created for true safety and care. It is mostly a way to safeguard against responsibility. At times, white people in the United States have been found innocent of crimes against Black and Indigenous people, the wealthy found innocent of crimes against the poor, corporations found innocent of crimes against people, water, and soil. For poor people, especially Black and Brown people, legal innocence is a less frequently awarded prize. For them, innocence is the benefit of the doubt, the far-reaching extension of humanity and compassion. If a young white kid sexually assaults a girl he knows, his legal innocence is the guarantee that his mistakes won't destroy his future (though there are no guarantees about hers). He is fundamentally good, just temporarily wayward. If a young Black boy commits

a petty theft, we wouldn't be surprised if he were shot by police outside his mother's home. In such a society, in which
innocence and guilt have no objective value, a justice system
and a belief system that award and seek innocence and guilt
do everyone in them a disservice. And yet we still use these
systems to arbitrate our conflicts, whether interpersonal or
societal.

When we strive toward proving our innocence, we protect
ourselves from really understanding our roles. No matter who
we are, when we construct an identity that has to be good or
right, we banish our shadows and our depths. James Baldwin said, "People who shut their eyes to reality simply invite
their own destruction, and anyone who insists on remaining
in a state of innocence long after that innocence is dead turns
himself into a monster."

What if we could do something different from having
innocence and guilt at the core of our conflicts? To give up
on this binary is not to erase the fact that we often hurt one
another in conflict—very much the opposite in fact. We do
hurt one another and sometimes in ways that are brutally uni-
lateral, for reasons that have nothing at all to do with one
another. We destroy parts of other people on a memory we
can't shake or a feeling we can't tolerate. It happens every day.
We enter conflicts unaware of the baggage we bring and how
we inflict it on one another. And yet, innocence doesn't stop
this and won't heal us. Neither will guilt. It only immobilizes
and isolates us further, and the unresolved hurt and resentment simmer inside us, waiting to erupt in our next disagreement. Instead, what changes us are the processes of making
amends, of incorporating another's reality into our own, of
knowing ourselves, our motivations, of being in practice that

interrupts our unconscious and violent flailing. What changes us is vulnerability, acknowledgment, and responsibility. Designations of innocence and guilt too often get in the way of repair.

What if, in resolving conflicts, we could move out of binaries and into a culture of accountability? Where we are proactively responsible for our actions and relationships. Where we are true to our internal values so that we don't need to be found out and called out to admit or address when we're wrong. Instead, we offer accountability because we are unsettled by our own actions or words. What if, instead of innocent and guilty, we could see ourselves as both harmed and harming, more or less honest, more or less able to be conscious when triggered, more or less manipulative, more or less caught in patterns, more or less willing to take responsibility for our own change? Could we then tend to the pain that is created in our breakdowns, instead of imagining that our denial and accusations will produce care and repair? Can we encourage all of us to learn inside of conflict and transform because of its occurrence?

I'm left with a question that I haven't yet been able to answer: What will it really take to believe in our and others' ability to change? Maybe the most direct question is: How do we begin to create this culture when there have already been so many betrayals?

Uprisings that spark movements for justice like Occupy Wall Street, #MeToo, Extinction Rebellion, #BlackLivesMatter, and #MaunaKea have been happening with greater frequency over the past decade or so. I imagine we could expect them to continue and grow as long as so many of us remain in denial about the needs and pain of others, unwilling to change and unskilled in addressing conflicts small and large. The conflict that an uprising or a protest shows us is the visible break-through, a rupture in an ongoing pattern of oppression, and presents an opportunity for our society, its systems and insti-tutions, to reckon with the experiences of the people within it, and to envision accountability that can change all of us. These public ruptures are a timeless human phenomenon, as people gather and revolt to show us the urgent need for change. The resistance to them, the reactionary forces that come, can make it seem impossible that we'll ever build a society capa-ble of transforming conflict into meaningful learning rather than trying to suppress it altogether. But as Frederick Doug-lass once said, "This struggle may be a moral one, or it may be a physical one, and it may be both moral and physical, but it must be a struggle. Power concedes nothing without a de-mand. It never did and it never will." A living society, one that doesn't doom itself to what it can't face, has to find a way to listen to the heart of movement.

Things fall apart but sometimes they are falling apart to show us who we were in the first place. Vulnerability can teach us, but it's necessary to have a culture that rewards rather than punishes it. A culture that encourages our tenderness more than it shames us. We can create these cultures in pockets, experiments in trust and revealing and repair. In our homes and organizations, in places where we can more safely see our-selves in process, as change itself, and we can see one another with the same potential for transformation. When we live like this, we'll see that conflict is not to be feared. We can fall apart and come back together all the time if, at our core, we believe in our development, that we grow, deepen, and mature. Really living our values decides the next shape we take.

CHANGE IS A PROCESS

A self that goes on changing is a self that goes on living.
—VIRGINIA WOOLF,
"The Humane Art" in *The Death
of the Moth and Other Essays*

I GOT TO SEE THE FULL RANGE OF SOUTHERN CHURCHES GROW-
ing up. My mother, for reasons still unknown to me, would
never join just one. We'd visit the multiracial Pentecostal
churches to make new friends, the Black Baptist churches
to see family, and the white Methodist churches when we
wanted to leave on time. Some had full bands, drummers,
lead guitarists, and hundred-person choirs. In others it was
us, the congregation, who sang with only an organist punctu-
ating the hymns. We went to churches repurposed from gas
station storefronts and megachurches with stadium screens,
churches where people fell out into the aisles possessed, and
others where people only moved as if on a track, up and down

according to instruction. Despite the differences in music, fashion, or food served afterward, every church, every Sunday, was in the business of transformation, and each had a ritual meant to get you to the other side.

After the welcome and announcements, and the shuttling in of late arrivals (cue our entrance), the music would begin. When done well, a choir primes and opens you. Harmonies, crescendos, are the relentless aural reminders of God's unwavering love and an invitation for your surrender into it. Even as a kid, or maybe especially, I could feel the portal start to open. The music would pry something in me away from my fear, something guttural, honest, pleading, wanting to be expressed. A good pastor moves you into this opening with fiery provocation, somehow taking a brief passage, in almost unintelligible language, and crafting a sermon that still manages to speak directly to you, your week of struggles on the job or your troubles at home. You are offered, through the Word, a path to a change so profound that you are like a baby being born all over again. I would watch the congregants, full on this possibility, step from between the pews and bunch at the foot of the pulpit, offering themselves up for this transformation. The church, as one sanctified body, prayed over them, swaying, shouting encouragement. And those too afraid or stubborn that week to let go of what bound them, gripped the pews so they wouldn't somehow lift off, too. Just like the rapture of the Book, the repentant were swept up by ushers and carried away to the back of the church. There, they were healed of their former pain, forgiven for their transgressions, and unburdened by the past. It was a mesmerizing show. These people, who looked no different to me on the outside than they had a moment before, had undergone a metamorphosis. It was a miraculous, instantaneous, and complete transformation that we were told only required us to want it badly enough to ask God for help and mercy. At its best, church is a calling to this other, nascent self—a calling out and into this rapturous change.

Church isn't the only place I've experienced this. In organizing and, particularly, during protests, I've had moments that echoed what I'd felt in church, where it seemed as though it all might change at once. Even ideas of liberation mirror to me, at times, the way I've heard people speak of the promised land: a perfect world just on the other side. Pouring into the streets breaks down the fourth wall and topples along with it our societal norms. I've found myself, arms linked with strangers, singing, chanting. Turns out that just outside of our comfort zones an odd but familiar intimacy with everyone is available to us. There's a power, too, that you can feel, buzzing, visceral, of what can happen when we commit to something together.

The revelation of church and the revolution of the masses reflect each other in a way. Both are the turning over of old paradigms that no longer serve us. They are both an opening to the prospect and, perhaps, the eventuality of a different world and ways of being, feeling, acting. Each is, in a way, a ritual. They are intended to bring about change, but they are also a reminder to the collective of the ongoing possibility that we can grow and live beyond our current fears. Rituals of rebirth are the sparks, the initiators, the doorways we move through to get started on the path of change. They are a glimpse into what could be.

We don't plant seeds on top of hard soil. We turn the dirt over, or, at the very least, we nestle the seed into the soft and welcoming belly of the earth. Something must crack open, make room for new roots to settle in and spread. Our bodies behave the way the earth does. We don't deeply change without first allowing ourselves to open. When I do bodywork with people and they lie on my table, I nurture these openings. When the time is right and safety is built, I might encourage someone into a breath pattern or movement of a part of their body that I've noticed they don't inhabit; it disorganizes them, brings suppressed energy back to them, more oxygen into their lungs. I might invite them with their anxious legs to kick a pillow I'm holding with all the force and rage they may have forgotten they have, or I might hold them tight enough so they can stop bracing and feel what they have been running from. In bodywork, we take someone just outside of their container and familiar feeling to show them there's room for the emotions or memories or impulses to flood in. When our bodies let go it can look any number of ways, sometimes wailing, teeth chattering, shaking, sometimes rolls of laughter. In this opening, where people feel emotionally disorganized, the practitioner reminds them, plants the seed, that what they love and envision makes feeling this odd, uncomfortable, sometimes painful sensation worth it. The vision is a guide that moves us through the unpredictable wave of sensations. The discomfort tells us to turn away, but there is a freedom we feel when we go through it. It is hard to describe to someone who has not experienced it, what it is for a body to open, but it is just as holy as falling before the pulpit and as righteous as a riot. It is the breaking of what binds. It is undoing so that we can become.

The summer of 2020 always felt to me like a collective embodied opening, so many people all over the world meeting outside the bounds. That fall I spoke on a Zoom panel with a few well-known guests in the realm of politics and healing. One made the comment that the protests and Black Lives Matter as a whole had resulted in nothing meaningful. No federal legislation like our civil rights predecessors had achieved. The comment raised my hackles, this audacity to be so dismissive, but it caused me to reflect. Why were we so quick to see movements in terms of success or failure, rendering them either useful or unuseful to the ways we measure progress? Hadn't it meant something to real people who exist now? Could the whole of that effort, the protests, the organizing that people did in their communities, be so easily disregarded? Was it not both an opening and a continuation of previous work?

Of course, I can see as clearly as anyone that there has been a significant and brutal backlash against what happened that summer. A concerted effort to roll back rights and reinstate law-and-order talking points that suffocate any real attempts to review and address police violence against Black people. A backlash that is not only a reaction to what happened, the swell of 2020, but an attempt to prevent something like it from happening in the future. But success or failure is not about what one summer was able to do, or even one movement. What determines the impact of any moment of human outrage or uprising is not only the magnitude of the opening, but what we do immediately after it. The relief you seek when you walk to the front of the church on Sunday is only sustained if you commit to the Bible studies held on Wednesday nights. Going out into the streets to protest is not a substitute for building relationships or making the close-in changes in the places you live, work, and worship. If the next day's actions do not leverage the power we summon in our openings, our calls to transformation, we get swept back by the force of things as they already are. There are moments of profound breakthrough that are so significant that we might call them radical, the pulling up from the root. But we can never forget that any moment of revelation is followed by a tomorrow, and tomorrow the work begins: the regular work, the attention and commitment to galvanize and sustain change over time, even amid the pressure of the familiarity and comfort of our previous habits. It's what we practice, what we offer into the world, what we do in the days that follow that turn our rituals into our reality.

In her 1993 novel, *Parable of the Sower*, Octavia Butler writes that change is the only constant in our universe:

All that you touch,
You Change.

All that you Change,
Changes you.

The only lasting truth
Is Change.

God
Is Change.

The novel begins in a dystopian landscape in the year 2024. The same year this book is published. Her predictions were prescient and alarmingly relevant to the timeline we find ourselves on. Her understanding of change, its ubiquity and force, gives us some insight into a phenomenon that is surprisingly hard to pin down. It is always and everywhere, each state flowing into the next. So constant that we might better understand change as the pace and process of life itself. This could be overwhelming to us, but is also, I think, an invitation to be involved in this process of transformation and embrace one of the greatest powers available to us.

Some changes, more powerful than human beings either individually or collectively, act on us: the march of time, gravity, the process of aging, our bodies' eventual death and decay. We don't control these processes and so we are at their mercy as they dictate the stages of our lives. But there is also change that we are capable of making. Some of it is and may seem small, greeting someone walking down the street, but like the butterfly effect, one small action has the potential to ripple and permeate, changing that person's day or yours and what comes next. As humans, together we can create change that is quite large, too, in positive and negative ways. Our modern lifestyles based on fossil fuel consumption have severely impacted weather patterns, threatening all planetary life. Our technological innovations, such as the ever-expanding field of artificial intelligence, are increasingly authorized to make and inform human-level decisions and will have an impact on global power and how life on this planet organizes itself. We can change so much when we want to.

Generally, though, we are not a society that does a good job of embracing change. We avoid the lessons of the opening and neglect the practice. The process that is change gets replaced with our desire for the immediate. Society sells and demands quick fixes. Split-second TikTok makeup transformations conceal the work and skill they require, the hours of practice and mediocre outcomes, the editing that changes a sleep-deprived face into a perfectly painted mug with the snap of your fingers. Instant transformation. Scrolling our news takes us from one crisis to the next; we are shocked for a moment and forget just as quickly. We confuse action that creates real, lasting change with hashtags and reposts. For some of us, it feels like all that we can and have time to do. We misrepresent change and it is misrepresented to us. The messiness of trying is edited out as though it is uninteresting. Before and after looks like magic, but what is most miraculous is found, if we know how to look, in what we see as lackluster and banal, the in-between where smaller failures and victories are stitched together through commitment and practice. For us to appreciate the process of any change we undertake would mean that we'd have to understand ourselves differently. To open ourselves to the truth that we are capable of changing. And that change is small steps and big steps, happening all the time.

WHEN I WAS IN THE seventh grade, I barely made the basketball team. Truth is, I did not make the basketball team. I had thought my moderate athleticism was enough to at least sit on the bench with my friends, but the coaches did not agree. So I stayed after school and begged them, promising to practice harder than anyone else. They must have pitied me because they reluctantly, but mercifully, offered me a spot on the B team. I played with full heart and dedication and, in the beginning, very little skill. I called my uncle's girlfriend, who was a star player on the high school team, and asked for her help. She met me at the neighborhood court and taught me the basics. We spent hours on the layup alone. It seemed simple to me at first, just jump and make a basket, but it was harder than it looked. To figure out which foot I pushed off with, when to lift up my knee, when to grab the ball and transfer hands. I was frustrated by what I thought would be easy. A layup, it turned out, was not one thing but several moves, a sequence that I had to practice repeatedly before I could do it without thinking. The same went for every other aspect of the game, dribbling, passing, stealing, making baskets. Eventually, though I was not close to being the best player on the team, I became a starter known for quick steals and running the ball back for points. At the end of the season, the coach named me best defensive player on the B team and drew on the certificate a picture of a stick figure grabbing a ball. I was proud. I'd become a better player. And I had learned something about learning and the process of change itself.

Repetition creates muscle memory and eventually embodiment, which means that when we do something often enough over enough time we will, at some point, no longer have to try to do it. It will come naturally. Most of our research on motor skills and muscle memory comes from sports science or early child development, but I don't think it's a far jump to assume that we can just as easily learn ways of relating to our emotions and engaging with one another that can become as embodied as our ability to make a free throw or swing a golf club. The key in each case is practice.

We are always practicing something, somatics teaches us. Everything that we do well now, whether it's knitting or showing up for our friends, judging others or working beyond our bodies' limits, took practice to achieve our current level of mastery. What is repeated, learned, practiced, becomes a part of who we are. Our society tends to think of practice as something we do to attain a skill like playing the piano or baking bread. We put in the effort and the hours, and we see progress. We consider it less when we think of our emotional development or the way we walk through the world, but of course we're practicing then, too. Every day, we practice our mood, our way of processing anger, or fear, or joy. We practice being receptive and open to others or closing ourselves off. We practice focus or distraction as escape. If we find what we practice effective, it will start to feel comfortable, like a familiar favorite coat, even as we watch some of these habits wreak chaos or disconnection. We don't always pay close attention and so we may not understand how good we have become at these habits and what effect they really have in our lives.

We have practiced, whether we realize it or not, who we are right now.

Recently, I watched my eighteen-month-old practice crossing the threshold of the front door. She tried with different foot heights, holding my hand and then refusing my assistance. She tumbled and picked herself up without shame or embarrassment, waddled past my "Are you okay?" She simply tried a different way the next time. I counted that she crossed the threshold twenty times before she was satisfied in her ability and moved on to playing with her toys or inciting me to tickle her. When she tumbles and tries again, she's learning more than how to climb. She's figuring out how not to dwell in frustration, that another attempt can lead to a sense of satisfaction and fulfillment. And when she holds on to my finger or refuses my assistance, she's embodying skills of trust and independence. As she practices, those emotional capacities will become ingrained in her alongside the skill of climbing.

Embodied practice is the call to intentionally and with awareness practice what we want to become. Very often, if we don't commit to a practice, name out loud our intentions, it can get drowned out by every other previous or imposed commitment we have. Our intentional commitment clears the room for consistency, making our intention into a practice rather than a one-time event. In practice, we encounter ourselves, our barriers and resistances. We work with them, listen to them, as they—and we—transform.

Practice can be small, subtle, but its impact can still be significant. It is the steady revisiting and refinement of our efforts. Any change we cull doesn't just arrive; it is made in the seemingly mundane and quiet return to practice, when no one is looking, a fire that catches from kindling. When I made a commitment to love, my practice was to maintain a breath-filled, soft chest when someone complimented or praised me. I had somehow practiced, without realizing, hardening my jaw and chest against kindness, preventing myself from ever receiving the feeling of love that was being sent my way. A practice can be as simple as that. To listen without trying to fix. To dance to a song that brings you joy. To attend a meeting a month. To create a nighttime ritual that cares for you the way you may have wished a parent did.

Practice is the portal for change. On a panel I facilitated recently on practice, political organizer and theorist Sendolo Diaminah said, "Practice is your center. What it is you do because it is life-giving and from it you have things to offer." Our vision shows us who it is we are becoming, what we long to build and create in the world. Our practice makes it so. If you want to become a writer, a dancer, a drummer, a good listener, or a present parent, you may find that you have a natural inclination, but practice deepens it, expresses what is you in it. When we fall in love with practice, we are less prone to the frustration and despair that come from repeating behaviors that don't work for us.

CHANGE DOES NOT TAKE PLACE OVERNIGHT. Our habits, whether they are about how we compulsively protect and hide or our training around supremacy and inferiority, were adopted through years of practice and reinforcement. We may have become embodied in injustice, in callousness, and in denial. We don't just let that go. To imagine that we can is a setup for quick failure. If we do attempt to just let that go, we end up pretending that we are more evolved than we are and living with a debilitating self-loathing, or we cynically give up on the idea that change is even possible—which drives us further from compassion for ourselves and real, embodied relationship with one another.

When I was twenty-seven, I had an epiphany. I realized that I was pretending to be much smarter, more astute, and even calmer than I actually felt. I aspired to all these things, but I wanted to be them now and thought "Fake it till you make it" was a grounded philosophy. I wasn't changing as much as I was performing. So I dropped it. I started to admit when I didn't know something. I emptied my bookshelf of books I kept there because they were the "right" books to own though I knew I didn't have any interest in reading them. Clearing the shelves was a way of letting my home life be a more honest reflection of who I was, of what I knew and believed in that moment. Only from that place could I begin to authentically and deeply grow and change.

It wasn't the first time I had wanted to change in an instant. As I was growing up, I sometimes wished I could start
over, be born again as my family wished, and then as I realized that was never going to happen, I started to wish that my
trauma would just disappear. When I started seeing a therapist, I hoped I'd be made anew after a couple of sessions.
It didn't happen, of course, but over time, as I centered the
practice of healing in my life, something else occurred, something more profound. My vantage point shifted. I learned that
I could exist and even thrive with my trauma as the space
widened between the pain of it and my response. It didn't
overwhelm me anymore. I saw that it was only when I gave
deep commitment to my personal transformation that real
change happened.

Meditation has been my longest-running intentional practice. I find my way to the cushion most days, sometimes reluctant, sometimes sleepy. On some days my thoughts are
jumping around, trying to escape or move away from some
emotional or physical discomfort I feel. That sinking feeling
in the pit of my stomach that I've been distracting myself from
is just there waiting when I'm still. I can sit with it or grab
greedily onto any thought that will whisk me far away. On
other days I stay with my breath or my gratitude and it takes
me straight down, like an elevator, into waves of feeling that,
each time, I live through somehow. It is hard to say that I've
gotten better at meditation per se, though I suppose in a way
I have. The daily habit of it is more than just accumulation.
Meditation has changed me, slowly, profoundly. When I get
feedback from a colleague now, I run less from it than I used
to. I don't move as quickly into the stories about how bad I am
or even how good. I can stay longer in the unformed feeling

and listen to what is really being shared with me and what it means. Practice isn't only helpful because repetition brings us closer to some kind of perfection, but because in each repetition we are met by our internal barriers, sometimes small and lurking, sometimes quite profound, that threaten the skill we are trying to learn. Practice is the recurring encounter with ourselves and the space to learn from it. The mundane is miraculous with the right attention.

"I FUCKED UP," MY CLIENT confessed over a Zoom call. We'd been working on his commitment of courageous leadership at work and, after hiding in the shadows and refusing positions where he would have to make final decisions, he'd co-led a campaign with someone on his team. At the launch meeting, he had choked in a presentation to the rest of their team. He couldn't figure out what to say above the bare minimum and fumbled answers to his teammates' questions. Afterward, his co-worker had asked what happened. She'd been empathetic, he said, but was disappointed, too. In our session, we danced along the edge of the shame spiral, careful not to drop in. We slowed down what had happened. When had his heart started racing? When had he begun the retreat into himself? When had the doubt that he could do it crept in? Could we find a way to make this bump in the road a lesson, an opportunity, but not a blockade? We were restoring his ability to tolerate being a learner again, putting himself out there, trying to change.

When my kid traverses the threshold of the front door, as far as I can tell there is no inherent correlation for her between her failed attempts and her worth. The concepts are unknown to her, freeing her up to learn. Her failure is not much more than an opportunity to refine her approach. We don't arrive in this world thinking that our inability to do something perfectly makes us unlovable. Yet, somewhere along the way, most of us pick up and hold on to this message. Shame gets wedged between our attempts and our learning.

Our capitalist culture, organized around nonstop productivity and unbridled, ever-increasing profit, doesn't leave much room for failure. So when we do fail, it comes with enough shame and social consequences that we overwork or over-extend in order to prevent it, and we scramble to blame others or hide it when it happens. We lose out on learning, on the change that comes from each iteration of attempts and failures. And how our own attempts at change change us. When we're allowed to fail, we're allowed to change.

I am sitting with this question of how we can be granted the space to deeply change, especially in the urgency of our time. How can we go deep but quickly? What in our cultures, in our values, and in our practices has to shift so that deep change is not suffocated by our impatience or perfectionism or shame? Culture is a hard thing to change. What we do and how supports both a logic and the goals of the society in which we live. But we can change culture in committed pockets, in community, where people set new aims, new visions, and create the rituals and practices to realize them.

Social movements have the complex role of inspiring and ushering in cultural shifts in the middle of what is currently not working. In them, we should practice what it is we are becoming. In a way, that is the mandate of movement, to practice the steps toward our visions, unless we only intend to change the window dressing. But like everything, we come to social movements and create them from our own embodiment. From what we've already learned and been taught. From what we think of ourselves and one another. And from the painful lessons that have wormed their way inside us, the questions about our worthiness. Many of us come to them, too, without any models of the kind of relationships, the kind of emotional dexterity and self-awareness, that our visions for change require.

A culture where we can change has to first be a culture that assumes belonging. When we see in our national politics a narrowing of who can belong, we are required to build in opposition a culture that is alive enough to value something more than homogeneity. A culture where the circle can widen enough to include everyone who is committed to care and reciprocity, no matter where they are on their path to change. I grew up hearing the discerning words often attributed to Zora Neale Hurston: "All skinfolk ain't kinfolk." A warning not to assume that just because someone looks like you or acts like you they are on your side. It has saved me a lot of confusion to know this discernment. The inverse of the lesson is powerful, too, and might actually be the harder one for us to grasp. That some of our kinfolk, defined by me as the people who are or could be on your side, might come from unexpected places.

Where people feel safety, where they feel they can belong, they can learn. Curiosity naturally emerges from a settled nervous system. A rose can grow through concrete, but it flourishes in the soil. Commitment alone has to be the price of admission into the beloved community we create—everything else we need can develop in it.

A culture where we could change would necessarily relinquish shaming as a tool of control. I know why we use it with our children and with one another when things go bad: It can, even if only temporarily, stop an action. But the underside is that it severs worth and holds belonging at bay. Shaming someone does not create the proper conditions for change, as it is only concerned with submission, which requires the internalization of badness. And badness, the sense that we are irredeemable, unworthy, is at the root of our most damaging and hurtful mistakes.

Forgiveness and grace have much more to offer any culture than we give them credit for. They are rare sightings these days, yet where I have seen them, when I've been offered them, I realize that they are not the weak, pitiful emotions of people who don't value themselves. They are the generous gift of people who know their worth cannot be diminished or compromised. When we offer grace or forgiveness, we refuse the false correlation between our worth and actions. But I'm not speaking about the kind of grace or forgiveness that coddles or panders. We don't forgive out of our own desperation for another person; we forgive to invite one another back into our highest selves, back into our commitments. There is an acknowledgment that someone has been wronged or hurt, and forgiveness extends the possibility of trying again. I have struggled my way through forgiveness and grace, just as most of us struggle with them because of how often our hearts have been broken and how often we've been betrayed. I think it's important for us to heed the warnings. Maybe eventually we can all learn to forgive far and wide, the way religions have taught. But for me to think of it that way is too tall an order. Maybe now we only need to forgive close in, nearby: the people in our families and our communities, the people we struggle alongside. Rather than denounce mercy, we try it in small doses. From there maybe forgiveness and grace spread and cover us, become more of the air we breathe.

In 2018, in the stretch of time after I'd left BLM, Kasha and I rented a camper van and drove to the Grand Canyon. One night under the stars, facing the gaping fissure of the canyon, I started to chant, "I failed, we failed," over and over until I began to sob. I kept crying until at some point I turned a corner and I felt myself grow calm. Here I was staring at this massive natural wonder that people drive miles to see, itself an erosion over time. It put things in perspective. When I got back home, I cataloged my learning and, somewhere, I started to dream up what I could offer back now. How could I take what I'd experienced and share it? I'd seen that our traumas made every hard thing harder. That our relationships fell apart too easily under pressure. That so many of us were animated by a pragmatism but not an infectious joy, not a love of the world and the people and the life in it. How could the way we lived inspire people to act as though their lives were worth saving? From my failure came a clarification of my purpose. To be a part of what Black feminist cultural worker and author Toni Cade Bambara meant when she talked about making revolution irresistible. The revolutions that happen inside of us, the change we need and long to make, and the revolution in how we build and maintain our world.

We will let one another down. We will fail and misjudge not only others but ourselves, too. We will try and give up, we will learn, and all of these are good signs, signs that we are alive. But we will, we can, and we must change.

COURAGE

With brave men there is always a remedy for oppression.
—FREDERICK DOUGLASS,
"What to the Slave Is the Fourth of July?"

THE POLITICAL POLARIZATION WE SEE EVERYWHERE AROUND US seems to me to be born out of a tremendously feral fear. This fear stretches to consume all of us, though in different ways. All of us can feel the walls closing in and the borders being erected. We feel it happening around us because these barriers, before they are built in the world, are first built inside of people: in some of us, and in the people we know. We sense that these walls are constructed to keep us out, or to keep people we love out, or to keep us locked in, away from the undesirable and threatening hordes of others. We know that these walls are built from fear. And even though lines are being drawn between us sharply, loudly, in the rhetoric we hear and repeat, we know somewhere deep down that these lines are uncomfortably subtle and temporary. We are all only a step away from the worst that is happening to each of us. It only increases our fear to know it.

A culture seized by this kind of terror and reactivity will cling to any form of power for protection, breaking the rules if it means self-preservation. It struggles to know or name its fear as fear or to imagine that change, though unfamiliar, could bring benefit or relief. We avoid talking about this fear at the core of our society and the cruelty it brings out in people, the way it infects people on every side of our common issues. It narrows our sense of connection and tinges our interactions with danger. The conversations we have with one another escalate quickly. Fear is present in every debate and inside of many so-called solutions. We are afraid and we are afraid to be afraid. This keeps some of us stuck in our incredulity or anger, while some of us nestle into complacency, hoping that if we are still enough, long enough, things will return to a normal we can recognize. Suddenly, we can see how the frog boils slowly. Perhaps we think that allowing ourselves to feel and name our fear would make the threats we face real. It's easier to pretend everything is fine if we are numb. Fear is an indicator, a way our bodies sense what happens next based on what has been, but our fear is not always right—neither in its assessment of what's taking place nor in its predictions. What happens from here can be determined by us, by what we allow ourselves to do with our fear. Is it possible to face it, feel it, rather than let our denial of it confuse us and make us vulnerable to stories that increasing separation and subjugation will create safety? Could this fear instead become courage, the kind that brings us closer to our lives and one another?

Maya Angelou once said that courage is "the most important of all the virtues, because without courage you can't practice any other virtue consistently." It's true, though I wonder if it can also be said that the other virtues—compassion, honesty, humility—require courage in greater sums now because of how far we've strayed from them, how unprofitable and dangerous our most altruistic instincts have become.

In one way, courage can be thought of as a skill that can be practiced; we can develop our ability to reach for courage in fearful moments. And in another way, courage is a state that we can learn to seek out. Eventually, we can almost crave it over comfort and certainty, knowing that courage gets us closer to authenticity, purpose, and genuine connection. Courage is the internal will to act despite pressure and risk. And when we take it on, when we are courageous, it changes us from who we were into who we will be.

A lot of us think of courage only in big, heroic gestures: superheroes swooping in and saving the day. I remember my father would tell stories about his time in the navy, and those stories, to me, became the epitome of courage. It was always masculine and militaristic and backed up and reinforced by everything television told me about the shape of courage. His stories were embellished, I know, because they changed over time, the stakes always growing higher and the other characters disappearing from the narrative, leaving him alone to his bravery.

I'm not necessarily denying the courage in some of those stories. There was risk, resolve, sacrifice. But courage doesn't only appear on battlefields. There are other acts of courage that we all too often overlook or minimize because we don't really understand or value what they require of us. When my mother made the decision for us to leave the home we lived in with my father, she planned it under the radar. Her best friend rented an apartment for us and we left one day, picked up our lives and started over. We didn't move far in miles, but our whole world changed when she built a home for us where we could feel safe. That was courage if anything is.

Healing itself is courageous. People stand on the edge for years, for a lifetime, contemplating if they will let themselves feel and face what they've suppressed. I remember the voicemail I got from my first-ever client. I remember vividly because of how nervous I was as a new therapist to receive it and how shaky her voice sounded over the phone. I had to play it several times to decipher her words; she wanted to talk to someone because she had not been feeling like herself. When she came for her appointment, I remember her walking wide-eyed into the office, afraid. She grabbed a pillow from the couch when she sat down and spoke to me from behind its protection. By the end of the session, she was crying and thanking me for listening. She'd always thought therapy was for other people, not her. But it was a huge relief for her to get things off her chest. I've heard some version of this sentiment many times over, and each time I realize that it takes courage for a person to pick up the phone and then to find their way to my office and risk being vulnerable with a complete stranger. At each step, the woman sitting across from me on the couch had swum against the stream of her own comfort and fear. She had resisted every internal message that she should remain small or hidden or feel shame for her own story. Healing, facing what is true, what we are afraid of, is one of the most courageous acts every time we do it.

In all his stories of battle, my father never mentioned fear other than to say the people he was with were afraid. In fact, he was courageous precisely because, unlike the others, he'd found a way to conquer fear, so it was no longer a part of the story he told. It's how most of us think of courage, as the absence of fear—how I thought of it, too, and why I never felt courageous. Even if we can acknowledge the presence of fear in a courageous act, we are mostly taught that it needs to be conquered, dominated—until we make it go away. That courage and fear coexist only in an eternal battle.

But courage is something more than its relationship to fear, and it's more than putting fear in its place. Researcher and author Brené Brown wrote on the etymology of courage that "*courage* is a heart word. The root of the word *courage* is *cor*—the Latin word for heart. In one of its earliest forms, the word *courage* meant 'To speak one's mind by telling all one's heart.'" What this tells me is that courage is not even mostly about fear. Courage is feeling what matters to us the most.

The team I work closely with has been looking at courage in the last few years as we've watched our nation's collective fear level skyrocket and escalate every conversation. At a recent retreat, we did a deep dive into courage, asking what our bodies know about it, this force we can generate inside of us that knows fear but doesn't succumb to it. How might we cultivate this virtue in each of us to affirm us in the hard moments, at times when we need it most? In our somatic trainings, we practice embodied courage, a courage that is feeling and aware, that doesn't shut down our sensitivity to take action. When someone is afraid to try a new move or gesture outside their comfort zone, we don't ask them to not feel the fear—because they already do. We don't ask them to wrestle their fear or make it disappear. Instead, embodied courage for us invites fear, in all its trembling, making room for it to include whatever might be there, the terror, the grief, the connection, and anything that makes it worth it to act in the first place. Fear is an alarm, one that we should listen to. One that tells us that something we care about is under threat and fills our bodies with the energy we need to do something about it. Sometimes that's to run and hide, other times it's to fight back. Whatever impulses we have are rooted in protecting what we love: our lives, one another, our planet. We care and so we are afraid. It makes sense then that we feel fear when we engage in a death-defying activity like bungee jumping, or when legislation restricting lifesaving medical interventions is passed. In each case, our bodies are perceiving some kind of threat. The protective impulse of fear can be our wisest message, but at times we want what is beyond our fear's dominion. We long for what only courage can help us reach.

Kasha's family has an intense philosophy about consciously and actively engaging fear and building courage that I respect but don't necessarily recommend for everyone. In our first three months of dating, Kasha took me on a secret hike known only to locals on her home island of Kauai. For that reason I won't describe it in too much detail, but I will say that this hike is treacherous and, I'm very sure, illegal. Technically, the "hike" is short, maybe two hundred feet at most, but it leads across a narrow ledge out to a boulder wedged in a cliff high above a canyon. When we got to the start, Kasha calmly offered a *pule,* a prayer, while I stood next to her feeling more terrified than I ever have been in my life. So afraid that once we began the hike, much to my embarrassment, I collapsed, twice; my shaking knees would not hold me up and my body threatened to evacuate its contents. When I thought I couldn't get to my feet again and said so, Kasha looked back at me with an expression I've never seen on another person's face, something simultaneously understanding and uncompromising. "Become bigger than the fear," she said slowly. She didn't tell me not to be afraid or try to assure me that there was nothing to fear. Instead, she was telling me to make room for my fear. Rather than become what the fear dictated, I could feel it and yet feel more. I breathed in and my contracted chest softened, and with the space that I had created I asked myself if I wanted to move forward. Turns out, I did. I wanted to see the view and I wanted the story of this moment and I knew that if I could walk straight out along this very narrow path then I would see something incredible. I zeroed my focus in on each successful step, allowing and incorporating the shaking that had lessened but still moved through me in waves. We made it to the boulder and sat there for an hour, laughing and just taking in the spectacular view of the canyon below. A new story started to upload: I'd done something I didn't believe I could, and I'd done it while being deeply afraid. No fear was defeated or conquered that day. I'd felt more fear than in most other times of my life. In courage we are still afraid, but we resist fear's contractions, we resist the suggestion that our shudders should be hidden. We stay open and let the fear move through us, letting ourselves tremble and shake and remembering that who we are and what we intend to do is sometimes big enough to face the risk.

Embodied courage allows us to harness the rush of energy that fear provides and instead of retreating, we act. We do something risky yet purposeful. We show up for therapy and start our journey toward healing. We begin an honest conversation that we've been putting off. We walk across a narrow ledge to take in an extraordinary view. When our bodies experience fear, our stress responses kick in, flooding us with hormones and impulses that help us to react. When we embody courage, feeling is our guide. We feel fear and use it, expand around it to include it. Just before and even after we contract into our protective postures, as I did when curled up on the cliff, there is an opportunity to choose openness instead, to breathe and allow the fear, and to use the energy that our bodies have produced to move, with all our shaking, toward a purpose or intention bigger than our fear will allow.

Remaining soft in the face of a million demoralizing and overwhelming incidents is an incredible feat of courage, too. Sometimes it takes courage just to be yourself. When I was twenty, I worked at a movie theater in Dallas and became friends with my co-worker Kiana, a Chamorro trans woman who performed drag on the weekends at the local gay club. Before her shows, I'd meet her at her house and listen to her stories about growing up in Guam while helping her get dressed. She was the first person who taught me anything about makeup or which bras to wear under sleeveless gowns. One night, I was looking over her shoulder in the mirror when she said, "You see how one side of my face looks different than the other?" I saw only then as she said it. Something about the right side of her face was always still and a little more serious than the left. "The doctors put a plate in that side," she said, and tapped just under her eye with an applicator brush. "I was walking home last year from the club and three men tried to beat me to death. I rolled under a car where they couldn't get me and that's how I survived. But they broke my skull and jaw." I knew why without asking. I understood then why she grabbed my hand and lovingly folded it close to her when we walked the three blocks from her house to the club, her singing at the top of her lungs, and I understood why she lectured me about never leaving without the people you came with no matter what. "You still go out, though." I said it as more of a statement than a question. "I'm not depriving the people of this beauty," she teased. She was not naïve. She didn't deny violence; she lived bigger than it. She lived her life anyway and taught me that there's a courage in being authentic that most of us never access.

It's courage when we insist on being ourselves in a world set against us. And it's through courage that we become ourselves. The people we are inside, sequestered beneath the norms of society or the trauma we carry, can find their way to the surface through the actions we take. When trauma does its work on us, breaking apart safety, belonging, and dignity, it can disconnect us from the sense that we are actors and that we belong in the world. We are instead the acted upon, and that belief can stay with us long past the initial injury. Courage is necessary for the healing process, central to it, because it is the first step we take to retrieve our agency. When we decide that we are also shapers of this world.

Courage is being willing to risk that same safety, belonging, and dignity—putting them on the line for the sake of something bigger: a vision, our principles, our power. It is not always, or even usually, well received by those we oppose, but we remember through it that there are things greater than complacency and comfort.

There was something else to Kiana's courage that I think rings true for those of us who summon courage especially in unjust environments. Courage is contagious and more powerful when we share it. One of the people I teach alongside explained in a conversation recently that courage naturally widens you. The person who makes a courageous act is a person concerned with something beyond their individual body. They act on behalf of a truth, a principle, authenticity, and it's this that inspires others to join in their courage. Many people in our world, threatened by our constrictive society, must practice courage because of who they are as a daily, even hourly, exercise. When more of us are courageous, when we stand up to what is unjust or untrue, we lighten one another's loads, we share the weight of the risk and create more safety for all of us. After that night at Kiana's, I showed up every time I could to prepare with her for her shows. We walked together from her house to the club and back and we both sang at the top of our lungs, an aural force field of joy and courage.

BLACK PEOPLE IN THE UNITED STATES have had to study courage, to enshrine it in our culture as a matter of survival. So powerful are the many examples of courage in Black freedom movements that one could speculate that part of what motivates the suppression of Black history is the threat these stories pose to any unjust status quo. They show us real courage that has love and concern for humanity at its core, capable of inspiring all of us. I think a lot about the internal constitution of these freedom fighters, imagining sometimes the way they breathed, how they stood against hurled insults and bodily attacks. I know the songs they sang in meetings to prepare themselves wove them together and gave them something to lean on when it got hard. Their courage was both full of feeling and sober about the risk, brimming with a magnanimous love. It was not a solitary, singular, macho courage that suppressed fear, though the stories have been told that way. It was a connective, generative courage that included and inspired people whose names we'll never know.

When I contemplate this kind of courage, I revisit Fannie Lou Hamer's story. One of the most brilliant and steadfast architects of the voting rights movement, she was also a food justice organizer who fought for Black farmers in a particularly exploitative food system.

It wasn't until 1962 that Hamer became aware of her constitutional right to vote, as white leaders in power in Mississippi had used any means possible—literacy tests, poll taxes, fraud, intimidation, and brutal violence—to prevent Black people from voting. After attempting to register to vote for the first time, Hamer was fired from her job as timekeeper at Marlow Plantation and forced to leave her family and live elsewhere. While she was staying with friends in Ruleville, Mississippi, their house was sprayed with bullets by white supremacists. Still, she managed to register to vote that year.

In June 1963, Hamer attended a voter registration workshop, traveling by bus to South Carolina with fellow activists. On the way home, after attempting to eat at a local café, she and six others were arrested, thrown into jail, and brutally tortured to the point of devastating and lifelong injuries by small-town cops in Winona, Mississippi. While forced to listen and watch as her friends were beaten, she sang hymns for their sake and her own. Hymns were their own technology that communicated and maintained a connection not only to God and one another in their harmonies but also to purpose in terrifying times. "When the darkness appears," she sang, "Lord linger near." Or "I shall, I shall not be moved. Like a tree planted by the water, I shall not be moved." Later, when asked how she continued her work for justice, she said, "I'm never sure any more when I leave home whether I'll get back or not. Sometimes it seem like to tell the truth today is to run the risk of being killed. But if I fall, I'll fall five feet four inches forward in the fight for freedom. I'm not backing off." The torture Fannie Lou Hamer faced did not turn her away; it mobilized her.

I have seen collective courage at work in organizing meetings, in the streets, and whenever people express their boundaries and say that enough is finally enough, that the ways things are structured have to change. When people are willing to put their bodies on the line, to spend their time outside of their lives figuring out how to bring about the transformations that we need. There, we can almost catch courage, as it spreads from person to person. This embodied courage does not override feeling or fear; instead, it catalyzes the energy they create into action. Our courage draws from the power of our vision to align our actions now. Courage helps us keep our commitments to the visions we see. Social movements are born from this mix of grief, fear, love, vision, and the courage it takes to change everything.

That we face the unknown is a condition of human reality, one that we can't escape. We have the capacity to predict but not the capacity to know. And for the foreseeable future, we will face unprecedented levels of uncertainty paired with potentially catastrophic risk: the threat of nuclear war, escalating climate change, violent and repressive regimes, inequality of opportunity and generational poverty, and the economic and social ramifications of artificial intelligence. It's true that the unknown we face may have taken on a more frightening quality, but instability and uncertainty have always been at the core of our human experience. Much of what we have been trained to embody is, on some level, different ways of living or coping with the unknown. For some people, this has meant choosing to control others to maintain a sense of power, while other people have prioritized staying under the radar, not rocking the boat, in an attempt to stay safe. No matter what we do, we can never know exactly what is in store. So why not meet it with curiosity? With authenticity? With feeling and with purpose alongside our fear? Courage can be an attitude toward the unknown. A disposition toward the future and a commitment to greet it as it is with all the hard decisions and fruitful opportunities it could hold.

As we look at the world around us, it is clear that we need large-scale change. But it will not happen without risking something of ourselves, perhaps by seeing ourselves honestly, by stepping up to lead, by speaking out, by feeling discomfort as we move outside our usual patterns. We shape change in such moments and transform ourselves in the process. Courage changes things and courage changes us. It's how we become. I have found that there is a "right-sized" fear inside any vision for change, and in taking courageous action we develop a part of ourselves that can talk back to and hold the fear without letting it lead. Guided—and inspired—by what we care about, we become able to express our courage and act.

The courage we need is the courage to fail and stay. The courage to reimagine every aspect of our social relations. The courage to relinquish grasping what was and build piece by piece a new structure for how and what we produce. The courage to exit the safety of our dying delusions. The courage to reach for one another. The courage to be honest. The courage to ask questions. The courage to listen. The courage to feel uncomfortable. The courage to be a part of the circle, to be fed by and to feed. The courage to surrender. The courage to know when our time is over and our roles have shifted. The courage to love and be loved.

We need courage, especially now. The courage to heal and change. The courage to come to terms with our history and the complexity of the challenges we face. The courage to lead and create. The courage to be nuanced when everyone around us is rigid. The courage to be thoughtful in our solutions even when we are faced with the most reactionary tendencies.

When we are courageous, we can do the unexpected and start to mold the world around a vision bigger than one produced by fear. Every inch of progress, every ounce of love, every truly meaningful action from here on out will happen through courage, not comfort.

LOVE AT THE CENTER

If love will not swing wide the gates, no other power will or can.
—JAMES BALDWIN, *The Fire Next Time*

SOMEHOW IT'S GOTTEN TO BE THAT TO TALK EARNESTLY ABOUT love is to reveal that you are not in fact a serious person concerned with the serious things of the world. Maybe it's why I've left this part for last. Or maybe it's that love somehow doesn't force its way to the front of any conversation about change. Not proud, it allows us to overlook it, though it is steadily there at the heart of it all. The first personal commitment I made, my vision, was a commitment to giving and receiving love. It feels a long time ago now, not so much in years as in how that commitment worked its way through my life.

When my child was born, my heart changed composition. It became so much wider and softer behind my ribs. Her smile, her presence, remind me every day that love has changed me fundamentally. More, if I'm honest, than any practice or therapy has so far. I see now that courage directs our actions, but it's love that gives our actions and our lives their meaning. My love for my child prioritizes things in my life. Suddenly, it's important to say words I'd feared saying before, important that I sort out our generational burdens. It is for her now that I'm so committed to what our culture, systems, and institutions could be, to how they can support and nurture life, to making a society where it is possible for her to flourish, together with those who come after.

Years ago in college while smoking a bowl in my dorm room, a friend asked, lost in her own high thoughts, "Hey, what is love anyway?" "What?" I replied, thinking the question was silly, obvious, but stopping short of being able to form the words to answer her. "Love is, you know, a feeling," I said eventually. "That's it?" she asked. "What kind of feeling? Is it enough that I feel it over here? How would I get it to you?" I remembered then that nineties song by Haddaway, "What Is Love," and suggested the answer might be hidden somewhere in it. Those were the days of Napster, so we quickly downloaded it, played it over her speakers, and scoured the lyrics for some insight. Turns out, Haddaway had no more answers than we did. He was only pleading, stumped by the same question, overwhelmed by the power of this thing he could not define. We sat back in silence. After thinking for a while, my friend offered, "Maybe love is when you're drawn to someone and want them to be close to you?" "Yeah, yeah, that's it," I said. "But sometimes we love them even when we know we can't be together." I thought it over and came to something that, a decade later, I found out was eerily similar to a phrase landed on by Saint Thomas Aquinas more than seven hundred years earlier: "I think love," I said, "is when we will another's existence." "Mmmm," my friend said, nodding, and we each fell back into our own worlds and our contemplations of love.

Willing another's existence could happen near or far, across time. It's not force or control, but a light and steady touch, a presence and attention. The steadiness of love, the will of it, is what gives it weight, distinguishes it from the thin love that Toni Morrison warns about in her novel *Beloved*. To will someone is a generosity of our own spirit, a shift from scarcity, a faith in connection. Love is a kind of reunification. As my friend pointed out that night, it's not enough for love to exist only inside of ourselves. It seems to long for gesture, for expression, to be infused into all that we create. Its expression is its power—and this frightens us, too. That night on my friend's floor, I ran the newly imbued word across the places where I might have experienced and known love in my life, and it showed me things I hadn't seen before, where love lived, and where I'd only received a paler, thinner version.

When I was growing up, there was a kind of love around me. My grandmother had a biting sense of humor and the gift of sight. She could see through you, and some of what she saw were your deepest insecurities. And she hardly ever hesitated to make a joke of what she found. Nothing was off limits. The last time I saw her alive, I attempted to look more feminine, even covering up my tattoos so I wouldn't upset her religious sensibilities. But as soon as I walked into the room she said, "You're a tomboy, and you ain't neva gonna change." I couldn't help but laugh. To be seen the way she saw me made me feel oddly secure; I always knew how she felt about me. On that same visit, I heard: "I didn't used to like you, but now you're one of my favorites." I kissed the top of her head, pocketed all the sweetness in what she'd said and left the barbs she wrapped it in. I never questioned her love (though maybe I should have). I only wondered why it could never come out pure, flowing. I knew it was there when she shoved twenty dollars into my palm on my birthday. She didn't have many twenty-dollar bills, so I tried every year to return them and she would grumpily tell me to stop blocking her blessings and walk away. I knew it when she picked me up on Saturday mornings to go thrift-shopping and we sat in the car afterward, drinking the milkshakes she loved and listening to gospel music like two little kids. I knew it when she'd grab me up in a rough hug and I wondered who she was fighting. Was it her own impulse and desire for closeness and softness?

It wasn't any easier for my grandmother to feel my love than it was for her to express her own. Maybe because of her, my family has a strong bond but struggles to put words or affection to our experience of and need for love. We struggle to let our guards all the way down. As a kid I was always sensitive. I wanted to talk about this love feeling I felt bubble up in me, but like a lot of Black families, we've been through things that we've never talked about openly, and when you talk about love you open a dangerous door. It stirs up memories of what we have not allowed ourselves to feel fully, and it reminds us that what is precious can be lost. So we bite our tongues rather than sing love's praises. Yes, we know selflessness and sacrifice whose origins are love, but most of us carry inside the question of whether we are worth the spilling over and the proclamation. Is anybody willing us to be here? Our love practice gets stunted like this.

Recently, the scholar and writer Alexis Pauline Gumbs

was a guest on my podcast, and I asked her, as I ask all my guests, to describe where we are in this moment, to locate us, to give us some bearing as everything seems to change around us. To my question, she responded, "Well, we are always in the unfolding of love. We are learning how to love as usual." That answer rang in my chest. Later, in reflection, I understood that love is the greater of what is always happening. And our strife, our disconnection, our disagreement, our denial, and our violence are the tantrums we throw against love's requirement that we understand, change, and become. I could see that love is always trying to unfold through each of us, but it is on us to dissolve the barriers that prevent us from loving, the barriers present in our own fear, in our ego and our bodies, and the barriers in our systems. We can love ourselves back to one another and back into this ecosystem if we try. Love is never very far if we invite it.

When I made my first commitment, that I wanted to be able to give and receive love freely, the first declaration I made toward any kind of change, I remember how my stomach jumped to say it out loud. Something caught in my throat. I wanted it but didn't know the first thing about living it. I started in the only place I had any real control and that was with myself. I took myself out on dates, doing exactly what it was I enjoyed most. When malicious voices critiqued everything I did or attempted to do, I interrupted them with affirmations. And I sang a lot of love songs to myself out loud in the car. It turns out there are very few love songs that are written for the sole purpose of expressing our love for ourselves. We have countless unconditional love songs for other people, lovers mainly, but most of the songs written about ourselves are regretful, apologetic, or boastful at the other extreme. So

I started singing love ballads intended for someone else to myself, envisioning my own face when I sang. Whitney Houston songs were especially well suited for this exercise: "Saving All My Love for You." "Run to You." "I Have Nothing." And of course, "I Will Always Love You." I don't sing well, but even that was part of the exercise, that singing them sincerely to myself would make something happen. One night, I caught myself in the rearview mirror and for the first time in forever I saw someone who was not flawed or broken, someone with an awkward beauty, someone who tried. I could see there was nothing to be ashamed about in my mistakes except perhaps how I denied them and tried to cover them up. I was no less or more lovable than my favorite people or anyone else in the world. The confusion that I couldn't ever be lovable had had a hold on me, an inherited confusion that I saw in the generations before me, that came from a society that ranked people's worthiness and value and ranked the people I loved the lowest. I saw now that I had always been lovable, and realizing that taught me about the love practice I deserved.

Kasha was my friend for many years before anything romantic happened. It wasn't until the passing of my grandmother, not too long after her grandfather had died, that we fell in love. It surprised us both, that our grief opened up the door for love. On a visit to see her in Hawai'i, she built an altar for my grandmother and her grandfather. They sat next to each other up there, framed and smiling, encircled in leis. She sat just below, and asked me to tell her stories about my grandmother. I was overwhelmed by the beauty of this invitation. Did I deserve to be loved like this? I shared and she listened with a steady presence. She gave me room to feel, and instead of being repelled by my vulnerability, she moved closer. The tears poured and she didn't rush to wipe them, just put a hand on my back, asked another question, or let the silence wash over us. When it came time for her to tell me stories of her grandfather, she held my hand tight and presented a complicated man, meticulous, reliable, who loved through actions but whose words only began to soften at the end of his life when his body gave way. I didn't know him but loved him, and caught fragments of the face I saw in his photo mosaicked in hers looking over at me. We were not only falling in love, we were in that unfolding of it; it was already here, a love that had room for generations. At the airport as I was leaving, I said to her, "I wish a love like this for everybody. Imagine what it could do."

A love like this disintegrates the things you have held on to and that have held on to you. When I became a therapist, I remember saying to a friend that it felt like I was getting paid to give someone the unconditional love they deserved. Certainly, there are skills involved other than providing the love that someone needs, but it is the deep affection, the care, that changes everything. When you mirror back to them that whatever has happened, whatever they have done, it can be faced, that allows someone to feel safe enough to untangle their stories and memories and find their lovability. To restore their capacity for love.

Love has the power, the potency, to transform us deeply—and love is hard. It is the greatest vulnerability we can know. When we express it, we have no assurance that it will be returned or wanted or reciprocated. And if we have had our hearts broken—by lovers, by family, by community, by loss—we know that just as love opens us up to the potential of immense awe and joy, it opens us up to immeasurable pain and grief. In *The Fire Next Time,* James Baldwin writes, "It is for this reason that love is so desperately sought and so cunningly avoided. Love takes off the masks that we fear we cannot live without and know we cannot live within. I use the word 'love' here not merely in the personal sense but as a state of being, or a state of grace—not in the infantile American sense of being made happy but in the tough and universal sense of quest and daring and growth."

Love is made even tougher when our culture hardens us against it. When we have been taught to equate love with weakness. When we seek the safe distance of hierarchies to protect us from the work of love. Our culture substitutes domination for the love that could exist between us. We seek power over one another and our environment in a way that perverts love into possession. There is no longer a place where love can be allowed to change us. Scrolling through TikTok the other day, I came across a post by a man saying that women want to be dominated, accompanied by spliced-together videos of other angry men to confirm his position. What terrified him so much, I wondered, to make it easier for him to post vitriol than to surrender to the love of a woman and discover, as an act of that love, what she longed for? What was he hiding at his core? The transgressive love of queer people undermines a society built on domination and exploitation. If some of us can love even where it is not advantageous or useful in the narrowest sense of our society, we threaten the myths of separation.

The idea of welcoming love as a means of relating—to ourselves and others—is challenging because it goes against all our training. There is a resistance to love in a culture that puts us down, shames us, and encourages us to run after other, less authentic versions of ourselves. But what if we were able to see ourselves as we are, to embrace our histories, resist shame, and still insist on taking action? That, to me, is a love practice.

In 2019, my friend Malkia Devich-Cyril lost her wife, Alana, to a quick-moving and vicious cancer. Before the cancer diagnosis, they had created a love practice for the ages. Their wedding, called A Love Revival, was the celebration of this profound and all-too-rare love. A love that changed the Malkia I'd known, a brilliant but combustible movement leader, into someone who spoke openly about the places their love had allowed her to go. When Alana passed, no one would have faulted Malkia for abandoning love altogether now that the seeming source of hers was gone. But she didn't. Instead, she's become one of love's greatest proselytizers and a sage on grief. She said in a recent article, "Joy is not the opposite of grief. Grief is the opposite of indifference. Grief is an evolutionary indicator of love—the kind of great love that guides revolutionaries." Love is extraordinarily powerful, even in death.

IN RECENT YEARS I'VE RETURNED to bell hooks's work on love. In her passing, we have lost one of love's champions, but in doing the work that love required of her, she has left us with a trove of questions, challenges, and insights for liberation and love. "There can be no love without justice," she said. "Abuse and neglect negate love. Care and affirmation, the opposite of abuse and humiliation, are the foundation of love. . . . It is a testimony to the failure of loving practice that abuse is happening in the first place."

It's not an oversimplification to say that many of us who fight for justice, whether conscious of it or not, are fighting also for love. I have heard as much from others and felt as much in myself. Being loved has felt like being coaxed out of my body's protection and received. And everyone I've known involved in social change carries the story or the face of someone who was not loved by the world. Before the grief and under the rage is love. We want to be loved on every scale, to have ourselves be loved enough that we are reflected in the world and systems we create. To be willed into existence and to be mirrored and protected. Love can bring us closer to the work of liberation.

In her writing, hooks warns us about the widening abyss of lovelessness that sits at the core of our society. The people who are convinced away from love, who are love starved and embarrassed to need something so tender and primal. The people who have bought into extraction and manipulation and don't realize that lovelessness is at the core of their greed. In the same way that oppression controls and directs trauma, it is set up to control the flow of love. When people around us are battered by the world, when our systems restrict and steal our time and energy, when trauma keeps us afraid of connection, it becomes harder to find our way back to love, for ourselves and one another, even as we long for it. When we believe what we are told, that instead of love, it is things, possessions, that give life meaning, we will fill our lives with what is disposable and never mature into a love practice that transcends objects or our individual selves. A culture that traumatizes its people and commodifies love as an antidote siphons love itself and its natural need for transmission.

hooks fuses love and power back to each other, teaching

us "that it is in choosing love, and beginning with love as the ethical foundation for politics, that we are best positioned to transform society in ways that enhance the collective good." Erich Fromm, a social psychologist and philosopher who wrote on ethics and love and whom hooks often quoted, said, "Those who are seriously concerned with love as the only rational answer to the problem of human existence must, then, arrive at the conclusion that important and radical changes in our social structure are necessary, if love is to become a social and not a highly individualistic, marginal phenomenon." Surely we know what the opposite of love can do. How politically advantageous it can be for a powerful few to cultivate hatred or contempt for individuals and groups of people. How distracted and misguided we can become when we pursue spitefulness and abandon love.

We turn away from love because of pain or illusions of power, and increasingly we see it as weak because we are afraid of what it requires. And honestly, we've seen that love doesn't protect anyone, that people who led with love died violently anyway. But it isn't love that was at fault. One of my favorite sayings from Malcolm X is this: "We need more light about each other. Light creates understanding, understanding creates love, love creates patience, and patience creates unity." Love is the light we make in the darkest of times.

The love this book speaks to, the love that it takes to heal, is a verb to be practiced out loud. It is the love found in listening. The love of hard truths. It is the love of showing up for one another when it is risky. It is the love of this inescapable web that compels us to care for the land and its sacred sites. It is a love that compels us to remember and relearn what has been lost. It's a love that lets us arrive, present to this time. A love that like the light from the sun provokes a flower into its full bloom. Love can do things no other force can. It is only through love that we are ever really changed. There's a love to be practiced that can tear down the walls of anything in its way. I believe in this destruction, but only for the sake of love. So that love can be set free in our relationships, in our institutions, in our cultures, and so that it becomes the shaper of our futures.

ACKNOWLEDGMENTS

This book has taught me many times over that you never really do anything alone. And for that, I'm so immensely grateful.

Thank you to the ones who came before, who made a way out of no way. Thank you especially to Harriet Tubman, Audre Lorde, bell hooks, James Baldwin, Toni Morrison, Grace Lee Boggs, and my grandmother Mary Haynie, each of whom guides me toward honesty and hope.

Thank you to each person who has trusted me over the years with the stories that live in your bodies. Every one of you has changed me profoundly.

Thank you to my teachers, friends, and teacher-friends: Spenta Kandawalla, Staci Haines and Richard Strozzi-Heckler, Vassilisa Johri, Liu Hoi-Man, and MawuLisa Thomas-Adeyemo for bringing me to this path. Denise Perry for giving me space to become and for being my family. Priya Parker, thank you for opening doors that I could not. Tarana Burke and Brené Brown, thank you for giving me a chance to speak. adrienne maree brown, Sonya Renee Taylor, Alexis Pauline Gumbs, and Hannah Dee for how you inspire me and for your loving witness and encouragement at each stage of this process. Mia Birdsong, Andrea Ritchie, and Angel McArthur for prayers and words of support when I most needed them. Alta Starr, Oscar Trujillo, and Jennifer Ianniello for your brilliance, for your insight, and for always being willing to meet me out on the edges of it all.

Thank you to my entire family. I love you and I hope I have honored our pain and our beauty.

Thank you to the Embodiment Institute team: Anesu Nyatanga, Bailey Jo Wadlington, Brooks Long, Courtney Sebring, devon de Leña, Justin Shepherd, and Maria McCorvey. Thank you for believing in this vision, for living it, and for holding it down in every way.

Thank you to my literary agent, Zoë Pagnamenta, for always having my back and for a clarity and guidance that never wavered.

Thank you to my Random House team, especially Jamia Wilson and Ben Greenberg, my brilliant editors. Thank you for letting this work move in you. And thank you for bringing out more from me with your curiosity and openheartedness. You are a dream team.

Thank you to Lindsey Tate, my editor and friend. You could see it when others couldn't. Thank you for listening and treating every word with love. And thank you for your insistence that this could be done. It's healed something in me to have had you by my side.

To Kasha, for everything you held, everything you postponed, every sweet word, and every real talk. Thank you for being the person I most love to think alongside and for bearing the early-morning and late-night deep dives. There's a bit of your love and wisdom in each page.

Amaya, everything is for you and you have brought everything meaning. Thank you.

And thank you, the reader, for making it this far.

NOTES

PROLOGUE: BEGINNINGS

xix   **a framework offered years earlier by** Kindred Southern Healing Justice Collective, "The Need," kindredsouthern hjcollective.org/wp-content/uploads/2020/07/Kindred -Healing-Justice-Collective-Needs-Statement-1-1.pdf.

xxiii   **in the billions** "Corporate America's $50 Billion Promise," *The Washington Post,* Aug. 23, 2021, washingtonpost.com /business/interactive/2021/george-floyd-corporate-america -racial-justice/.

CHAPTER 1: VISION

8   **has us at just ninety seconds** John Mecklin, ed., "2023 Doomsday Clock Statement," *Bulletin of the Atomic Scientists,* Jan. 24, 2023, thebulletin.org/doomsday-clock/current -time/.

11   **an article about why humans tend** Paul Ford, "Why Humans Are So Bad at Seeing the Future," *Wired,* May 17, 2021, wired.com/story/why-humans-are-so-bad-at-seeing-the -future/.

18   **In PTSD research, it is referred to** Matthew Ratcliffe,
      Mark Ruddell, and Benedict Smith, "What Is a 'Sense
      of Foreshortened Future'? A Phenomenological Study of
      Trauma, Trust, and Time," *Frontiers in Psychology* 5 (Sept. 17,
      2014): 1026.

CHAPTER 2: HEAL

28   **Native psychologists like Eduardo Duran** Eduardo Du-
      ran, *Healing the Soul Wound: Trauma-Informed Counseling for
      Indigenous Communities* (New York: Teachers College Press,
      2019).

28   **In her groundbreaking book *Trauma and Recovery***
      Judith Herman, *Trauma and Recovery: The Aftermath of
      Violence—from Domestic Abuse to Political Terror* (New York:
      Basic Books, 2015), 10–32.

29   **Bessel van der Kolk has highlighted** Bessel van der Kolk,
      *The Body Keeps the Score: Brain, Mind, and Body in the Heal-
      ing of Trauma* (New York: Viking, 2014).

31   **Complex trauma, first introduced** Judith Herman, "Com-
      plex PTSD: A Syndrome in Survivors of Prolonged and Re-
      peated Trauma," *Journal of Traumatic Stress* 5, no. 3 (1992):
      377–91.

36   **work of writer Sonya Renee Taylor** Prentis Hemphill
      (host), "The Body with Sonya Renee Taylor," episode 1,
      July 27, 2020, *Finding Our Way,* findingourwaypodcast.com
      /individual-episodes/s1e1.

CHAPTER 3: FEELING AND THE BODY

51   **Physicist Fritjof Capra, in his book** Fritjof Capra, *The
      Turning Point: Science, Society, and the Rising Culture*
      (London: Fontana, 1990), 56.

55   **"emergent self-organizing process that"** Dr. Dan Siegel,
      "The Self Is Not Defined by the Boundaries of Our Skin,"
      Dr. Dan Siegel (blog), Mar. 17, 2014, drdansiegel.com/the
      -self-is-not-defined-by-the-boundaries-of-our-skin/.

66 **the works of Resmaa Menakem** Resmaa Menakem, *My Grandmother's Hands: Racialized Trauma and the Pathway to Mending Our Hearts and Bodies* (New York: Penguin Books, 2021).

67 **"We need ritual because it"** Malidoma Patrice Somé, *Ritual: Power, Healing, and Community* (London: Arkana, 1998), 53.

68 **"The white fathers told us"** Audre Lorde, *Sister Outsider: Essays and Speeches* (Berkeley, Calif.: Crossing Press, 2007), 38.

CHAPTER 4: REMAPPING RELATIONSHIPS

74 **Maya Angelou's poem "The Mask"** "Maya Angelou Poem 'The Mask,'" YouTube, Russell Jones channel, Aug. 8, 2010, youtube.com/watch?v=UT9y9HFHpU0.

90 **defines trust this way** Charles Feltman, *The Thin Book of Trust* (Bend, Ore.: Thin Book Publishing, 2009), 74.

CHAPTER 5: ENGAGE WITH THE WORLD

103 **Martin Luther King, Jr., once defined** Martin Luther King, Jr., *The Autobiography of Martin Luther King, Jr.,* Clayborne Carson, ed. (New York: Grand Central Publishing, 2001), 324.

109 **Arendt called on philosophers** Hannah Arendt, *The Human Condition* (Chicago: University of Chicago Press, 2018).

CHAPTER 6: EXPANDING OUR WE

120 **"Each of us, helplessly and forever"** James Baldwin, *The Price of the Ticket: Collected Nonfiction 1948–1985* (Boston: Beacon Press, 2021), 702.

120 **"The opposite of Othering"** john a. powell, "Us vs Them: The Sinister Techniques of 'Othering'—and How to Avoid Them," *The Guardian,* Nov. 8, 2017, theguardian.com /inequality/2017/nov/08/us-vs-them-the-sinister-techniques -of-othering-and-how-to-avoid-them.

124 **"I said suppose . . . horses began"** Emma Brockes, "Toni Morrison: 'I Want to Feel What I Feel. Even If It's Not Happiness,'" *The Guardian,* Apr. 13, 2012, theguardian.com /books/2012/apr/13/toni-morrison-home-son-love.

129 **Haraway talks about the need to create** Donna J. Haraway, *Staying with the Trouble: Making Kin in the Chthulucene* (Durham, N.C.: Duke University Press, 2016), 4.

135 **"We need acts of restoration"** Robin Wall Kimmerer, *Braiding Sweetgrass: Indigenous Wisdom, Scientific Knowledge, and the Teachings of Plants* (Minneapolis: Milkweed Editions, 2013), 195.

CHAPTER 7: THINGS FALL APART

154 **"People who shut their eyes"** James Baldwin, *Notes of a Native Son* (Boston: Beacon Press, 1955), 159–75.

156 **as Frederick Douglass once said** Frederick Douglass and Moses Dresser Phillips, *Two Speeches, by Frederick Douglass; One on West India Emancipation, Delivered at Canandaigua, Aug. 4th, and the Other on the Dred Scott Decision, Delivered in New York, on the Occasion of the Anniversary of the American Abolition Society, May, 1857* (Rochester, N.Y.: C. P. Dewey, 1857).

CHAPTER 8: CHANGE IS A PROCESS

162 **"All that you touch, / You Change"** Octavia E. Butler, *Parable of the Sower* (New York: Seven Stories Press, 2016), 3.

174 **she talked about making revolution irresistible** Thabiti Lewis, ed., *Conversations with Toni Cade Bambara* (Jackson: University Press of Mississippi, 2012).

CHAPTER 9: COURAGE

177 **"the most important of all the virtues"** Anne Ju, "Courage Is the Most Important Virtue, Says Writer and Civil Rights Activist Maya Angelou at Convocation," *Cornell Chronicle,* May 24, 2008, news.cornell.edu/stories/2008/05 /courage-most-important-virtue-maya-angelou-tells-seniors.

179 **"*courage* is a heart word"** Brené C. Brown, *I Thought It Was Just Me: Women Reclaiming Power and Courage in a Culture of Shame* (New York: Gotham, 2007), 19.

186 **her work for justice** Maegan Parker Brooks and Davis W. Houck, eds., *The Speeches of Fannie Lou Hamer: To Tell It Like It Is* (Jackson: University Press of Mississippi, 2011), 74–83.

CHAPTER 10: LOVE AT THE CENTER

191 **thin love that Toni Morrison warns** Toni Morrison, *Beloved* (New York: Alfred A. Knopf, 1987), 193–94.

193 **"Well, we are always in the"** Prentis Hemphill (host), "Remembering with Alexis Pauline Gumbs," episode 7, Oct. 19, 2020, *Finding Our Way,* findingourwaypodcast.com /individual-episodes/s1e7.

196 **"It is for this reason"** James Baldwin, *The Fire Next Time* (New York: Dial Press, 1963), 95.

197 **"Joy is not the opposite of"** Malkia Devich-Cyril, "Grief Belongs in Social Movements. Can We Embrace It?," *In These Times,* July 28, 2021, inthesetimes.com/article /freedom-grief-healing-death-liberation-movements.

197 **"Abuse and neglect negate love"** bell hooks, *All About Love: New Visions* (New York: William Morrow, 1999), 53.

199 **"it is in choosing love"** bell hooks, *Outlaw Culture: Resisting Representations* (New York: Routledge, 2006), 294.

199 **"Those who are seriously concerned"** Erich Fromm, *The Art of Loving* (New York: Harper & Brothers, 1956), 132.

199 **"We need more light about"** John Henrik Clarke, ed., *Malcolm X: The Man and His Times* (Trenton, N.J.: Africa World Press, 1991), 304.

INDEX